END-PAPERS

Designs on end-papers are from a metalworker's pattern book, c. 1785, in the Department of Prints and Drawings. Front end-paper, p. 121; back end-paper, p. 125.

E.2259-1913

FRONTISPIECE

BEDSTEAD

Japanned wood, with modern yellow silk curtains.
About 1755.
W.143-1921
This bed, which came from the Chinese bedroom at Badminton, Gloucestershire, is based on three designs (Pls. XXVI, XXXI and XXXII) which appeared in the first edition of Thomas Chippendale's *Director*, published, with a list of subscribers, in London in 1754. The owner of Badminton, the fourth Duke of Beaufort, was one of these subscribers, so it seems not unreasonable to attribute the bed to Chippendale. One of the designs (Pl. XXVI) was omitted from the third edition of 1762 and, as the Duke died in 1756, the Chinese bedroom and its furnishings was probably newly fitted up in 1755.
It is typical of the rococo whimsy of the period that the design for this bed could just as well have been applied to making a Chinese summerhouse or temple, and Messrs Edwards and Darley's *New Book of Chinese Designs* which also came out in 1754 shows many such *Chinoiserie* confections.

Victoria & Albert Museum

GEORGIAN FURNITURE

A new edition revised and edited by
Desmond Fitz-Gerald

London   Her Majesty's Stationery Office   1969

© *Crown copyright 1969*
Large Picture Book No. 1
First published 1947
Second edition 1958
Third edition 1969

SBN 11 290027 5*

Printed in England for
Her Majesty's Stationery Office
by Norman Brothers Limited
Cheltenham and London

FOREWORD

This pictorial survey of Georgian furniture was originally made in 1947 by Mr Ralph Edwards when he was Keeper of the Department of Furniture and Woodwork. A revised edition appeared in 1958.

The present edition, while based on the original conception, has been considerably enlarged, rewritten and entirely replanned. Account has been taken of the fact that some of the finest examples of the Museum's Georgian furniture are described and illustrated in the series of Picture Books on *Tables, English Chairs, Chests of Drawers and Commodes* and *Desks and Bureaux* which has appeared over the last few years. It was decided that the same ground should not be covered.

A different selection of furniture is therefore provided in the present work. Examples from Osterley Park House are also included, while several recent acquisitions are illustrated – in some cases for the first time.

The intention has been to show the various kinds of furniture that were produced during the Georgian period, and, by arranging the subjects in something approaching a chronological order, to reflect the rapid stylistic developments of the time.

This edition has been prepared by Mr Desmond Fitz-Gerald, of the Department of Furniture and Woodwork, assisted by Miss Gillian Wilson.

1969   JOHN POPE-HENNESSY *Director*

INTRODUCTION

This volume provides a general pictorial survey of the Museum's collection of English furniture between the years 1715–1825. Throughout the period, furniture was designed in relation to interior decoration, which in its turn was most intimately related to its architectural environment. The series of Georgian panelled rooms in the Museum serves to suggest this decorative background, but a comprehensive view of its development must be sought in the diminishing number of town and country houses of the Augustan age which still retain their original character. The contents of Osterley – pronounced by Horace Walpole to be 'the palace of palaces', with a drawing-room 'worthy of Eve before the fall' – are the property of the Museum; and there we are able to realize the full measure of Robert Adam's achievement (Figs. 86–88).

The century between the death of Queen Anne and the accession of George IV is marked by rapid growth and development in English national life. Before it closed, the traditional organization of society, dating back to the Middle Ages, had yielded to urbanization and industrial enterprise based upon machinery. This change, known as the Industrial Revolution, had a far-reaching effect upon all the applied arts, and inaugurated an era of mass production. The restless enquiring spirit of the eighteenth century finds expression in its decoration and furniture. It was a time of creative energy and ceaseless experiment. Within its limits several distinct styles, inspired by conflicting ideals, rose and waned. To each a fickle and capricious society accorded a welcome soon to be withdrawn. There was an avid demand for novelties and the latest mode. Baroque extravagance gave way to Rococo fantasy, and that to a refined Classicism, which, at the end of the century, was superseded by an archaeological revival based on a close study of the remains of the ancient world.

DECORATION AND WOODWORK

In the great Palladian houses of the Early Georgian period the decorative treatment associated with the later English Renaissance and Sir Christopher Wren was largely transformed by Italian influence. This movement owed much to cultured and travelled amateurs, like Richard Boyle, third Earl of Burlington, while Colin Campbell's *Vitruvius Britannicus* (1717) sums up its aims. The state rooms in houses built by Campbell, Kent, Leoni, Brettingham and others versed in this Italianate style, were of great size and height. In them a lavish use was made of decorative painting, stucco and marble. The vogue for the Baroque painted decoration introduced by Verrio and his school in Charles II's reign persisted into the succeeding age, and ceilings continued to be adorned with naked deities and allegorical subjects, which are often distinguished by great facility and brilliance of handling. An example can be seen in the work of Antonio Belluci on the ceiling of the room designed by Gibbs from Henrietta Place, St. Marylebone (Figs. 13-14). Many other foreign painters came to England in the 1720's – men such as Pellegrini and Marco Ricci – while a whole school of Italian *stuccatori* frequently worked alongside them on the plaster-work that adorned the ceilings and walls. Indeed, this room also illustrates this kind of collaboration, for the elaborate plasterwork is probably by Artari and Bagutti, craftsmen who frequently worked for Gibbs.

When panelling was introduced, instead of the wide bolection mouldings of the previous age, the panels were 'fielded', *i.e.* chamfered at the edges and set in a plain framework, or recessed within carved borders. Cedar, walnut, and mahogany (as at Houghton for Sir Robert Walpole) were sometimes employed, but early in George III's reign, according to the architect Isaac Ware, deal or pine had become 'almost the universal timber' for panelling.

In these panelled rooms decoration was concentrated on the salient features. The chimney-pieces, of marble or carved wood, with architraves, pilasters or terminal figures supporting the mantelshelf, continue the tradition of Inigo Jones; indeed, some of them were almost transcripts of his designs. These chimney-pieces are often found with an upper stage enclosing a picture. The doorways have richly moulded surrounds and a convex frieze with central tablet supporting a pediment.

Alcoves and wall niches are freely introduced, while the pine woodwork was invariably painted; olive green, blue, buff and brown being the colours most commonly employed. Later, white of a shade approaching ivory was considerably used, the salient detail being enriched with gilding. This type of Georgian interior is well represented in the Museum by the room from Hatton Garden (Fig. 19), which conforms to the rule laid down by Abraham Swan that 'there must be sufficient spaces left plain so that the ornament in proper places may be more conspicuous and may have their desired effect'. This room and the other rather more ornate example from Henrietta Place already mentioned, were stripped of successive layers of paint, which obscured the carving, soon after they had been acquired; they have since been repainted. Unfortunately, before the repainting, the decorators of the 'twenties took up this stripped and then pickled mode as being correct and therefore, inadvertently, the Museum was responsible for the host of naked pine panelled interiors that still disfigure houses on both sides of the Atlantic.

In many great houses the walls of state rooms were of painted plaster with lavish enrichments of masks, festoons and trophies executed, mainly by Italian stuccoists, in bold relief, the upper stage of the chimney-piece being decorated in stucco or marble with figure compositions adapted from classic originals. Walls were also hung with silk damask, velvet and tapestry; while papers printed from wooden blocks, or with the designs drawn and coloured by hand, were popular as a cheaper substitute. Some of these papers were copied from Chinese originals, and a room from Wotton-under-Edge, Gloucestershire, dating from about 1740, is an example of such imitation. Specimens of Chinese papers from which such copies derive, can be seen in the Print Room. Some of the best known cabinet-makers of the period carried out interior decoration on a considerable scale: thus, Chippendale's bills contain many items for supplying wallpapers.

From about the middle of the century, Rococo influence becomes perceptible in the carved enrichments and stucco decoration of 'houses of consequence'. They lose their heavy Baroque character, becoming noticeably lighter and more fanciful in treatment. The 'capricious ornament' against which Colin Campbell had inveighed was carried much further and became the mode. Interlaced scrolls in endless variety with a medley of naturalistic ornament – rocks and shells, foliage, and flowers – formed the decorative repertory of this new style, which derived from the *rocaille* ornament of Meissonier, Pineau, Cuvilliès, and other contemporary French designers. Highly sophisticated, despite its apparent resort to nature, it aimed at a kind of logical disorder and the consistent exploitation of asymmetric curves.

French inspiration is very apparent in the lavishly carved and gilded enrichments of the splendid Music Room (Fig. 54) which comes from Norfolk House, St. James's Square. Its decoration, however, only superficially recalls that of the contemporary drawing-room formerly at Chesterfield House, Mayfair, which was built by Isaac Ware for the fourth Earl of Chesterfield and completed in 1752, for at Norfolk House the panels are *Régence* in character and it is probable that they were imported from Paris. It is interesting to compare the marvellous free Rococo cartouches inset into the somewhat old-fashioned Inigo Jones type ceiling of the Music Room with the more ponderous Italian plasterwork of the previous generation as exemplified at Henrietta Place (Fig. 14).

The mid-century also saw the arrival of the 'Chinese taste', which was used experimentally in lesser rooms. And here the extreme of bizarre invention is attained. Sir William Chambers, the first English architect to visit China, sought to suppress the wilder manifestations of this exotic craze – 'the extravagant fancies that daily appear under the name of Chinese'. The Gothic style, a travesty of medieval art applied to structures of lath and plaster, was taken up by Horace Walpole and a group of dilettanti of whom Richard Bentley and 'that great genius', Sanderson Miller, were the most influential. The Lee Priory Room designed by Wyatt for another member of the Walpole circle, Thomas Barrett, is in the Museum (Fig. 82). Soon this style found its way into pattern books, and the 'bastard Gothic' of such designers as Batty Langley, for all its essential absurdity, possesses a kind of preposterous charm.

About 1760, these strange aberrations gave way before a newly wakened enthusiasm for classical remains, evoked by the discoveries at Pompeii and Herculaneum and by such publications as Stuart and Revett's *Antiquities of Athens* (1762). The dominant spirit in this movement was Robert Adam, who, soon after his return from Italy in 1758, effected a complete revolution in architecture and the allied arts. He substituted for the ponderous conceptions of the Palladian school a decorative convention based on the remains of Greek and Roman buildings, and on the grotesques and arabesques of Cinquecento ornament – all adapted to new purposes with astonishing resource. Though Sir William Chambers, James Wyatt, James Paine, Thomas Leverton, and other fashionable architects embraced similar classical ideals, Adam's ascendancy was such that within a brief period 'everything was Adamitic, buildings and furniture of every description'. The effect upon interior decoration was profound. A complete harmony was obtained in the design of the ceiling and walls, the pattern of the carpet, the furniture and fittings, everything being brought within the compass of a single style, logically conceived, and consistently worked out. Halls and principal living-rooms were often circular or elliptical, broken up by large alcoves, and with ceilings domed, vaulted, or groined. Stucco decoration was now executed with extreme delicacy and finish, the designs drawing freely upon the repertory of classic ornament collected from Italian encaustic paintings and bas-reliefs. This light and elegant 'Grecian' treatment provoked some protests from the admirers of the more virile 'Roman' manner, and was stigmatized by Sir William Chambers as 'filigrane toy-work'.

Decorative painting was brought into the closest stylistic harmony with the plaster enrichments, imparting warmth and colour to rooms. The compartments of ceilings, overdoors, and panels were filled with classic subjects, arabesque designs of Renaissance character being also used with excellent effect. As at the beginning of the century, most of the best decorative artists were Italians: Zucchi, Cipriani, Bonomi, Biagio Rebecca, and Angelica Kauffmann all obtaining wide patronage in England.

Mass production is already foreshadowed in some of the processes employed. Much of the plaster ornament was cast from moulds; scagliola, an imitation of coloured marbles in composition, was used for columns and floors, while marbling and graining were resorted to, at the close of the period, to enhance the effect of inferior woods. Sporadic attempts were made, however, to revive the ambitious mural painting of earlier times. John Mortimer carried out an elaborate scheme of decoration on the coved ceiling of the saloon at Brocket Hall, Herts., the work being completed after his death by Francis Wheatley. At Drakelowe Hall, Derbyshire, Paul Sandby decorated the walls of the dining-room with mountainous landscapes and foliage in *gouache*. The alcove end of this room, dated 1793, is now in the Museum (Room 40). These are rare instances of true mural painting. Most of this late eighteenth-century decoration consists of canvases painted in the studio and let into the ceiling or applied to the walls. It was an age of substitutes, and much of its ornament violated the nature of the material imitated; composition strengthened with metal cores allowing of a delicacy of treatment impossible in carved wood, much of the ornament on the chimney piece and door architraves was cast in pewter and then painted over.

Refined simplicity is the keynote of interior decoration in the last years of the century. It is seen at its best in the work of the brilliant architect, Henry Holland, who between 1795 and 1800 built Southill for Samuel Whitbread and enlarged Carlton House for the Prince Regent. Holland may be held to have introduced the French version of classicism favoured by the Prince and his circle. He had an almost infallible sense of proportion, and a remarkable power of imparting fresh life to a decorative convention already outworn.

With the end of the century the influence of the French Empire style achieved a final victory over the lingering Renaissance tradition, represented by the later followers of Adam. A new and more intense study of classical precedents set in. A Greek revival was sponsored by architects, while Egyptian remains were added to the sources of inspiration. Napoleon's African campaign and Denon's great work, *Voyage dans la Basse et la Haute Égypte* (1802), helped to establish this vogue; but it was discouraged by Thomas Hope, the leading English designer of decoration and furniture who warned its votaries that as Egyptian symbolism was 'seldom intelligible' in ordinary households, it should be sparingly used. This revived enthusiasm for the antique produced a frigid, pedantic style with a strong bias towards archaeology. The free use of enrichments in interior decoration was considered frivolous and ruthlessly suppressed by the more austere protagonists of the movement; Sir John Soane pronouncing that ornaments appropriate to the temples of the ancients 'became puerile and disgusting in English houses'. Under this ban, cornices, columns, and entablatures were often included; so that such interiors, stripped of traditional structural elements, now present a meagre and forbidding aspect. At the time, this appearance was mitigated by wall-

7 ❧ Georgian Furniture

papers and window draperies, often in primary colours and decorated with Greek, Roman, or Egyptian patterns. Few of these still survive to give an adequate impression of this strange archaeological style, which its votaries held to be the final expression of civilized and enlightened taste.

FURNITURE

Some years after the death of Queen Anne the simple and dignified furniture associated with her reign was superseded by a new style, baroque in conception and based upon French and Italian models. On the repeal of the heavy import duties, mahogany from the West Indies gradually replaced walnut as the fashionable material. Gilding was freely used to enhance carved ornament, while the ostentatious mirrors, side-tables, and stands characteristic of the period were of pinewood overlaid with gesso and gilt.* This grandiose style was developed by architects for a small governing class, and was at first confined to a few palatial houses. Among the chief structural elements are columns, architraves, and entablatures, with terminal figures and heavy scrolled supports. Favourite ornaments are swags and wreaths of flowers, lion and human masks, and broadly handled acanthus leaves. The chief exponent of this new manner of furnishing was William Kent (1684–1748), who, after studying in Italy, was introduced to the fashionable world by the third Earl of Burlington. He soon became an arbiter of taste and achieved a reputation in several branches of art. Kent was the first Englishman to bring movable furniture within the scope of his architectural schemes. He designed not only houses but much of their contents for the Duke of Devonshire and the Earls of Burlington and Leicester; while elsewhere he was responsible for a great part of the interior, though

---

* The process employed throughout the eighteenth century is known as 'water gilding'. On a thick skin of size and whiting, a coating of clay, generally red or blue, was laid. After it had been rubbed down and moistened with water the gold leaf was applied to this ground. In the later oil gilding process a preparation of boiled oil (gold size) is used instead of water. This process is cheaper and more expeditious, but oil gilding discolours in a comparatively brief time. In gesso gilding the surface was thickly coated with the preparation, in which the more delicate ornament was carved. Oil gilding of mirror frames is allowed by Stalker and Parker (*Treatise of Japanning and Varnishing*, 1688) and the accounts show that it was practised in the decoration of Ham House in 1638.

another architect had been employed. At Holkham, Houghton, and Rousham, his furniture may still be seen in the setting for which it was carefully thought out. It was planned to harmonize with Palladian architecture and baroque decoration, but it is incongruous, at least in its more extravagant forms, when associated with other styles. Characteristic of Kent's style is the monumental side-table from Coleshill (Fig. 23). The Museum also possesses a sarcophagus-like chest (Fig. 11), the eagle side-table (Fig. 27) and a mirror probably designed by him for Frederick, Prince of Wales (Fig. 26). The origins of the Kent style have much of their basis in Roman Baroque furniture of the late seventeenth and early eighteenth century but also a very important source is the engraved designs of Pierre Le Pautre and Jean Berain. Indeed the Bateman chest just alluded to is directly based on one of Berain's engravings.

Some of the earliest engraved designs for furniture published in England conform to the Kent style and illustrate it in a modified form adapted to the homes of the middle classes. Among the most important are the designs for side-tables, cabinets, and bookcases given in Batty and Thomas Langley's *City and Country Workmen's Treasury*. Another was William Jones's *Gentlemens or Builders Companion containing a variety of useful designs for doors, gateways, peers, pavilions, temples, chimney-pieces, slab tables, pier glasses, or tabernacle frames, ceiling pieces, etc.* Both these works appeared in 1739, and with others issued about the same time are the productions of minor architects or builders. They are merely complementary to the architecture illustrated and suggest no technical knowledge; indeed, two of Langley's side-tables are exact transcripts from designs by Nicholas Pineau, the celebrated French sculptor and decorative artist. The side-table (Fig. 42) is exactly based on one of these designs in Langley's *Treasury*, Plate CXLII.

The names of a number of the more prominent craftsmen of the Early Georgian period have been handed down to us, mainly through the preservation of their bills. John Gumley, a well-known cabinet-maker and glass manufacturer, was in partnership with James Moore between 1714 and 1726, the firm carrying on business in the Strand. It supplied the Royal palaces with mirrors, chandeliers, frames for tables, and a variety of gilt and walnut furniture. The word 'Gumley' is carved on the frame of one of the tall, gilt wall mirrors at Hampton Court Palace; while Moore's name appears on a set, consisting of a gilt gesso table and candlesticks, also at the Palace. Such inscriptions are rare on English furniture of the eighteenth century, though printed trade labels, advertising the makers' wares, are sometimes found affixed to cabinets, chests of drawers, and tables. Reliable attributions can be made to Moore on stylistic grounds as his furniture is highly idiosyncratic. The table top shown in Fig. 12 is typical of this kind of furniture. The chest or coffer of sarcophagus form (Fig. 11) is a most characteristic example of the lavish Baroque phase, and here some of the decorative motives are also reminiscent of Moore. Benjamin Goodison, of the Golden Spread Eagle in Long Acre, was largely employed by the Crown in George II's reign, and to him may be attributed the gilded mirror made for the Prince of Wales (Fig. 26).

Towards the middle of the century this ponderous style gave way to one which was its complete antithesis. Something has been said above of Rococo decoration, and a similar indulgence in caprice and fancy distinguishes the furniture of that age. Among the earliest indications of the change are the designs for mirrors and wall-lights, published by Mathias Lock about 1745, in which the lively spirit of French *rocaille* is cleverly rendered. Lock was a draughtsman of rare ability and is now recognized as the main pioneer of the Rococo taste in English Furniture. But it is in the first edition of Chippendale's *Director* (1754) that the new style is seen fully naturalized and combined with excursions into the contemporary Gothic and Chinese tastes. Chippendale invented and drew many of the designs in his *Director* personally, but Lock and his collaborator H. Copland, who were in Chippendale's employ at the time were undoubtedly responsible for a considerable number of the designs. Those in the Rococo style are largely derivative, owing much to the leading French decorative artists, but in the process of adaptation they acquired an unmistakable national idiom. Many extravagant fancies remained unrealized, or were freely modified in the course of manufacture. Lacking the audacity and invention of the *rocaille*, a certain good sense and sobriety characterizes most of the English versions. The more resolute attempts to emulate French exuberance are represented by a dressing table (Fig. 39). Among the examples which represent the style in its more coherent and successful form are one of a pair of mirrors (Fig. 66), which are probably from Chippendale's workshop; while the tea table (Fig. 73), with its faultless proportions and delicate ornament, shows that at the height of Rococo influence, elegant simplicity was sometimes achieved.

In range and variety the *Director* represented a new departure, for it included not only ceremonial furniture but a great variety of types for ordinary domestic use. Some of the most important designs were intended to be gilt and japanned. Of this treatment the japanned bedstead from Badminton (*see* frontispiece) is a capital instance. It is, moreover, an extreme example of the Chinese vogue, and recalls a plate in the *Director* (1st Edition, Plate XXXII). This bedstead, probably made by Chippendale for the fourth Duke of Beaufort, was formerly in a room 'finished and furnished very elegantly in the Chinese manner'. The bedstead was provided with curtains of Chinese silk or chintz, and an approximation of the original appearance has been recently restored to this pagoda-like fantasy. Among the comparatively few objects which correspond with published designs is an organ case (Fig. 61), and the 'ribband-back' settee (Fig. 56) is a rendering of a celebrated design in which the author took a special pride.

Owing to the great reputation of his book, Chippendale's name overshadows that of his contemporaries, and he was formerly held responsible for all the best mahogany furniture of this period, much of which must in fact be the work of other hands. His genius as a craftsman, or at least, as the organizer of a highly successful business, is proved by the contents of such houses as Harewood and Nostell Priory, where his productions are authenticated by receipted bills. But it is significant that, though the period of his activity saw large orders for furnishing the Royal palaces, Chippendale's name does not occur in the accounts of the Lord Chamberlain's Department and he was rarely, if ever, patronized by the Court. Prominent among the craftsmen employed by the Crown were John Bradburn, Benjamin Goodison, and the partners William Vile and John Cobb. A mahogany bureau-cabinet, supplied by Vile and still at Buckingham Palace, has all the characteristics of the so-called 'Chippendale style' and is of a quality unsurpassed by that famous maker. In other pieces Vile's personal taste is more clearly apparent. He favoured wreaths clasped with acanthus and pendants of fruit and flowers; the quality of his productions is of the highest order, and as an exponent of the Rococo style, pride of place must henceforth be assigned to him, though much of the carving on his pieces was executed by John Bradburn. An important pedimented medal cabinet by Vile, probably ordered for George III or his father was added to the Museum's collection in 1963 (Fig. 34), its mate being now in the Metropolitan Museum in New York. They were separated over a hundred years ago and it is likely that both units belonged to a much larger structure of architectural form. The quality of the carving is superb.

The success of the *Director* led to the publication of other works, conceived in a spirit of rivalry. Of these, Ince and Mayhew's *Universal System of Household Furniture*, published in parts between 1759 and 1763, is the most important. Though the public are admonished to cultivate propriety and a 'peculiar neatness through the whole house', this advice is discounted by the extravagance of the designs in the Gothic and Chinese styles. The plates which are made 'as easy as possible to the capacity of every workman' by the addition of profile mouldings, include a few varieties of furniture not illustrated in the *Director*, notably tea tables with tripod stands (Fig. 58). William Ince appears to have been the dominant partner, signing the majority of the designs. On their trade label the partners announce that they sell 'French furniture' consigned from Paris, while the notes to the plates in their book are printed in English and French, an indication that they hoped to secure a foreign market. In this aspiration they were not alone. Giles Grendey of Clerkenwell exported 'japanned' furniture, and the Museum possesses a couch, japanned red with gilt enrichments, which formed part of a set made earlier in the century by Grendey for a castle in Spain.

Furniture in the Rococo style has been traced to the designs of several of Chippendale's contemporaries, such as Ince and Mayhew, Johnson (*see* Fig. 65), and Lock and Copland, who, besides collaborating for the *Director*, published a number of independent works. Robert Manwaring specialized in designing chairs, and an example in the Museum (Fig. 75) recalls types shown in his book, *The Cabinet and Chair Makers Real Friend and Companion*. Attributions to individual makers, in the absence of bills, are hazardous, for pattern-books were widely circulated and supplied models to the trade. That the high standard of craftsmanship which distinguishes this period was not confined to the capital is proved by the knee-hole writing table (Fig. 47) which is inscribed in faded ink on the bottom of a drawer (the third to the left of the knee-hole), 'David Wright, Lancaster, Fecit, August 11, 1751'. This is one of the rare instances of an autograph inscription on a piece of English eighteenth-century furniture, and is of particular interest in view of Pennant's statement in 1772 that Lancaster is 'famous in having some very ingenious cabinet-makers settled here'. For at least a generation the furniture for the London branch of the well-known firm of Gillow had been manufactured in the town (an early nineteenth century sofa in the Museum (Fig. 136) is an example of the firm's later work). Though mahogany was the usual material during the Rococo phase of design, a large quantity of walnut furniture was produced down to the middle of the eighteenth century.* Keyboard instruments normally continued to be made with walnut veneers, as the spinet by John Crang testifies (Fig. 46)—this instrument is of a characteristically English form, and of a type that was much exported to the Continent and America.

The classical revival, with which the name of Robert Adam will always be associated, dates from the early years of George III's reign, and first attained definite expression in the homes of a few great magnates. In 1762 Adam produced his plans for providing the Duke of Northumberland with a suite of rooms at Syon 'entirely in the antique style'; and there, as in other houses, furniture formed an integral part of the general scheme. The Museum possesses sections of Adam's Glass Drawing Room from the Northumberland town house that originally stood in the Strand (Fig. 91). The style was

---

* Throughout this period the furniture made for the governing class is divided by a wide gulf in the quality of the materials employed, excellence of carving and technical 'finish', from that supplied to ordinary citizens. Distinction of design deriving from a long-established tradition and the makers' innate appreciation of form is a more widely distributed attribute, and is often found in furniture of relatively mediocre craftsmanship.

free from any marked archaeological bias and was essentially eclectic, the repertory of ornament being drawn from the same sources as the contemporary mural decoration (*see* above). Indeed, so consistent was the treatment that in houses equipped under Adam's supervision the same patterns and decorative motifs are frequently found on ceilings, carpets, and inlaid furniture. Among the details derived from classical sources – the 'Ancient works in the Baths and Villas of the Romans', in Sir John Soane's phrase – are the anthemion or honeysuckle ornament, so often used for ornamental borders, oval pateræ, medallions, and festoons of husks. Other prominent decorative ingredients are terminal figures, ram-headed capitals, vases, and urns. In wall furniture such as cabinets and bookcases, there was a return to the architectural pediments and entablatures of the Palladian school; but the proportions were more carefully studied and the mouldings more accurate. The furniture produced under Adam's supervision was of a ceremonial character suited to the 'parade of life'. A characterististic arrangement, which may be attributed to him, is the sideboard flanked by urn-surmounted pedestals. In houses designed by Adam, a group of this kind took the place of the isolated side-table hitherto employed for serving food. Torchères and tripods, painted or gilded, were also freely used in saloons and drawing-rooms to support vases or candelabra. A pair of such stands from 20 St. James's Square, which was perhaps the finest of Adam's town houses, are in the Museum Collection (Fig. 95a). The more delicate ornament is carved in pinewood and applied on a ground of mahogany; on the removal of modern paint and gilding, the original colour was revealed. These pedestals formed part of the furnishings of the Eating Room, the delicate blue and ivory-white matching the decoration of the walls. The interior decoration of Osterley Park House, carried out between 1761 and 1780, shows some of Adam's most felicitous designs and clearly demonstrates the development of his style during that period (Figs. 86–88).

Tapered and fluted supports, rectangular or of baluster shape, supplanted the cabriole leg as being more in harmony with the severe and simple lines of the new style. Many chairs of this time have oval-, heart-, or shield-shaped backs with an openwork splat, or symmetrically arranged bars of tracery. Upholstered chairs closely resembled the contemporary French models, and were covered with tapestry, damask, or leather (needlework was no longer fashionable), the woodwork being gilt or japanned.

Despite the force of Adam's example, 'the electric power of this revolution in art' (which incidentally was inaugurated before the parallel development in France) did not become manifest immediately. In the third edition of Chippendale's *Director* (1762) the Rococo style still predominates, and there is no trace of classical influence. Yet, before his death (1779) Chippendale had assimilated the new ideals and, in association with Adam, produced furniture of extraordinary distinction. The work done at Harewood House between 1772 and 1775 'stands out among the few masterpieces of English furniture, comparable in technical brilliance with the finest achievements of the French cabinet-makers of the eighteenth century'; and henceforward Chippendale must rank as the supreme exponent of the Neo-Classical style, in contrast to the former conception of his achievement. In some of the most notable of these productions the art of marquetry is revived, and attains a technical excellence hitherto unparalleled. A variety of new exotic woods, stained and shaded, were employed with remarkable decorative effect, while satinwood was used by Chippendale as early as 1770. Several good specimens of this style of marquetry are in the Collection, notably a commode by John Cobb, a cabinet designed by Robert Adam for the Duchess of Manchester, a small fitted dressing-table of elegant design and a commode (Figs. 103, 97 and 106a and b). Lacquered, or japanned, decoration was also restored to favour, especially for bedrooms, and Oriental panels were sometimes cut up to form commodes. An excellent example with brass mounts and owing much to the French influence is in the Museum (Fig. 77). Many of these costly pieces of inlaid or japanned furniture have finely chased ormolu mounts, the English production of such wares being stimulated by the establishment of Matthew Boulton's factory at Soho, near Birmingham, where he is said to have kept thirty-five chasers at work.

The degree of Adam's responsibility must not be exaggerated: others co-operated with him in effecting the change. The Museum possesses a large collection of designs for furniture 'made and for the most part executed during an extensive practice of many years in the first line of his profession by John Linnell, upholsterer, carver, and cabinetmaker.' This collection* contains designs for a large variety of furniture, including chairs, settees, state beds, commodes, mirrors, and picture frames. They range from the Rococo and Chinese to an original interpretation of the classical style. The notes show that Linnell (died 1799) was employed in a number of great houses, and was making furniture for Kedleston before Sir Nathaniel Curzon became Lord Scarsdale in 1761. He has now emerged as one of the most prominent makers of the period, and several fine examples have been traced to his designs. A cabinet in the collection (Fig. 100) which closely follows an existing drawing by him typifies the elegance of his compositions. A similar ability to vary his style was shown by Lock, who, after being associated with the plates for Chippendale's *Director*, designed with considerable success in the classical manner. Another maker of high standing, now almost forgotten, was William France, who was employed by the first Lord Mansfield at Kenwood and Bloomsbury Square between 1768 and 1770, in association with Chippendale and Adam. France supplied most of the furniture to Kenwood, including large gilt pier glasses, which still remain in the house, and a mahogany reading-table now in the Museum (Fig. 85). Nor was Adam the only fashionable architect concerned in the production of furniture. In the Department of Prints and Drawings will be found designs for mirrors and candelabra by James Paine (1725–89), the builder of Brocket Hall; while there exists furniture designed by Sir William Chambers, James Wyatt, and 'Athenian' Stuart.

The principles demonstrated by this group of architects and designers, working in the third quarter of the eighteenth century for extremely wealthy clients, are found adapted to the use of cabinet-makers in general in the trade publications of the late eighteenth century. In Hepplewhite's *Guide* (1788), the Neo-Classic style, associated with Adam, is modified and skilfully translated into vernacular terms. The declared aim was 'to unite elegance and utility, and blend the useful with the agreeable'. Though the designs vary in merit, they show that from the diffusion of classical ideals a manner

*Department of Prints and Drawings; pressmarks W. 1–7, W. 8a & b, 92. D. 26.

of furnishing, simple, rational, and elegant had resulted. Many of the objects illustrated were to be made in satin-wood, inlaid with various woods; while for other designs japanned (*i.e.* painted) decoration is recommended, 'a fashion that has arisen within these last few years'. In fact most of the japanned decoration of this time is merely varnished paint, the varnishes composed of gum, lac and other constituents on a prepared ground being no longer employed.

Hepplewhite's *Guide* disowns originality and claims to have followed 'the latest or most prevailing fashion' in preference to mere novelty. Thus, the style represented is not so much the creation of any one individual as an expression of collective tendencies; indeed, it is doubtful if George Hepplewhite was personally responsible, for he had been dead two years when the book came out and it was published by his widow. It seems likely that the Hepplewhite firm supplied designs for cabinet-makers rather than making furniture themselves. No bills from the firm are known, nor can any furniture be definitely assigned to it. Designs scarcely distinguishable from those of the *Guide* are to be found in the *London Cabinet Makers' Book of Prices* (1788). A few plates in that catalogue are signed 'Hepplewhite', but the majority are by Thomas Shearer, who also incorporated them in his *Designs for Household Furniture*. They include bureaux, bookcases, and sideboards, while he seems to have specialized in dressing-tables and washing-stands, of which the fittings are extremely ingenious.

A large number of craftsmen at this period are identified by bills, or by pieces of furniture bearing their trade labels. George Seddon, a cabinet-maker and upholsterer was established from about the middle of the century at 150 Aldersgate Street, 'a house with six wings'. In 1768 the *Annual Register* records the destruction by fire of London House, 'now occupied by Mr Seddon, one of the most eminent of cabinet-makers of London. The damage is computed at £20,000'. An inventory of the firm's stock in 1789 shows it to have been worth nearly six times the amount of their loss. From the diary of a German lady who visited the establishment in 1788, we obtain an exceptionally full description of this Georgian cabinet-maker's business.* Four hundred journeymen were employed, and the staff included upholsterers, carvers, gilders, mirror-makers, workers in ormolu and locksmiths. In the showrooms were chairs, stools, and sofas 'made of all varieties of wood'; while the patterns for other varieties of furniture ranged 'from the simplest to the most elegant'. Seddon was 'for ever creating new forms', which implies that he was not only a maker but also a designer. Despite the vast scale of this undertaking, very few of the firm's productions have been identified. Under the name of Seddon and Sons, the firm was still prominent early in the nineteenth century, when it received large payments for the furnishings and decoration of Windsor Castle. George Seddon himself died in 1801.

The most important trade publication of the last half of the eighteenth century is Thomas Sheraton's *Drawing Book*, a work so ambitious and comprehensive that it has caused the author's name to be associated with most of the furniture produced in England between 1790 and 1800. Yet this classification is misleading. There is no reason to suppose that Sheraton, who was trained as a 'journeyman cabinet-maker', ever possessed a cabinet-maker's business of his own, or made any considerable quantity of furniture. His professed intention was 'to exhibit the present taste', and that some of the designs represent models already in use is suggested by various remarks in the Introduction. But Sheraton's imagination and technical knowledge were responsible for many improvements and modifications. Though it is possible to regard the designs in the *Drawing Book* merely as a representative collection of the types in vogue, if they are compared with the illustrations in Hepplewhite's *Guide*, published only three years earlier, it will be seen that the style has been largely transformed in the interval. Much of the credit for this result must be given to Sheraton. That his book exerted a powerful influence is suggested by the fact that nearly six hundred and fifty cabinet-makers from all parts of England subscribed for it. The designs of this period are graphically illustrated by the drawings of individual pieces in the Gillow Records (now in the Westminster

* *Tagebuch einer Reise durch Holland und England von der Verfasserin von Rosaliens Briefe*, Offenbach, 1788 (Marie Sophie von la Roche). *Sophie in London* (1788), translated from the German by Clare Williams, 1933, pp. 173–75.

Public Library) and these show how one firm could disseminate what is known as the Sheraton style. While elegance and refinement are the chief characteristics in the designs of this period, practical cabinet-making, called by Sheraton 'one of the leading mechanical professions in every polite nation in Europe', reached the zenith of excellence. This technical mastery is particularly noticeable in such matters as carcase construction, dovetailing, and the running of delicate mouldings. The finest furniture of the late eighteenth century was made of satin-wood, often combined with a variety of costly veneers. Some admirable examples of this kind are included in the Museum collection, the inlaid satin-wood bookcase (Fig. 126) being worthy of special notice. There was also a large output of furniture made in soft wood and painted to accord with the coloured walls and soft-toned hangings of contemporary rooms. Such japanned furniture was essentially decorative, and some of the more important specimens are painted with figure subjects and mythological scenes, after the designs of Angelica Kauffmann, Zucchi, or Cipriani. For chairs, rectilinear shapes were coming into favour. Lattice-work or vertical moulded bars are characteristic designs for the backs, while the legs are often turned and the framework fluted.

Until the death of Adam in 1792, the influence of the Adam style was still paramount on furniture; though his designs were freely adapted by cabinet-makers, their classical origin was often obscured in the pursuit of luxury and feminine grace. The modified version of the French *Directoire* and Empire styles, which became current in England around the end of the eighteenth century, covered the whole field of decoration and furniture. In its later phases it was carried out with rigid consistency, and was animated by a doctrinaire, archaeological spirit. The aim was to reproduce the exact forms of antiquity where precedents existed, as for couches, chairs, and candelabra; and for objects unknown in the ancient world, the great majority, to provide designs which should be fully consonant in character. Thus, by a free use of symbolism and ornament, often exploited in the most incongruous positions, every variety of domestic furniture was made to conform to the prevailing ideals. Figuring prominently in these designs are archaic lions (Fig. 135), winged sphinxes, hocked animal legs (Fig. 134), and emblems such as the 'fulmen of Jupiter'.

These were said to be drawn from 'the best antique examples' of three civilizations – the Roman, the Greek, and the Egyptian; but during the last phase of this so-called Regency style, 'Grecian severity' became the ideal. The inordinate use of symbolism, of which the significance was naïvely expounded in contemporary pattern-books, is characteristic of the desire to gratify the insatiable demand for novelties at all cost. Classical prototypes were diligently studied by the more erudite designers, and many of the chairs of this time, with their wide top rails and sweeping curves, approximate very closely to the Greek *klismos* found represented in vase paintings and Athenian reliefs.

In the furniture he designed for Carlton House and Southill, Bedfordshire, about 1800, Henry Holland finely interpreted 'the beautiful spirit of antiquity'; but to render the letter also was the avowed aim of the more ardent enthusiasts. The designs of Thomas Hope, whose *Household Furniture and Interior Decoration* (1807) was 'a consistent archaeological fantasy', show the style disciplined by scholarship and a sense of fitness. In the preface it is claimed that the chief merit of the furniture illustrated 'consists in the chastity and play of its contours'; while breadth and repose of surface, distinctness and contrast of outline, and the opposition of plain and enriched parts 'are calculated to afford the eye the most lively, most permanent, and most unfading enjoyment' – an apt summary of the attributes of the style at its best. Its wilder extravagances are represented in George Smith's work, *Household Furniture* (1808), and Sheraton's incomplete *Cabinet-maker's Encyclopaedia* (1805). A comparison of kindred objects, one in the Neo-Classic, the other in the Regency style, will tell us more than any description of the contrast between them in spirit and outlook (cf. Figs. 92 and 134).

At this period it was held that 'mahogany, when used in houses of consequence, should be confined to the Parlor and Bedchamber Floors', while satin-wood, rose-wood, and tulip-wood, were considered appropriate to boudoirs and drawing-rooms. Much of the carved ornament was bronzed, or gilt, and metal inlays and appliqués were freely used (Fig. 140). The fondness for striking contrasts of colour, characteristic of the early nineteenth century, is well shown in the secretaire veneered with zebra-wood and mounted with bronze terminals in the Egyptian style (Fig. 137). The sofa made by the firm of Gillow already alluded to (Fig. 136), is another characteristic object, a free adaptation of the type associated with David's famous portrait of Madame Recamier. A library table with lion supports, from one of Hope's designs (Fig. 135) represents the style in its more rational form, and shows that masculine dignity and monumental character were achieved by its abler exponents.

The archaeological character of some of this furniture is apt to give a rather unfavourable impression of contemporary taste, but we should remember that it was designed in relation to a carefully considered decorative scheme, and cannot be fairly judged in isolation. The finest examples of this later classical revival show no sign of the rapidly approaching decadence and go far to excuse the wilder aberrations in this vein.

21 ❦ Georgian Furniture

BOOKS AND DESIGNS

A large number of contemporary source-books, together with modern works on Georgian furniture and decoration, may be consulted in the Library of the Museum. Original designs may be seen in the Print Room of the Department of Prints and Drawings.

The following Museum publications also contain information about Georgian furniture: *A Short History of English Furniture, English Chairs, Tables, Chests of Drawers and Commodes, Cabinets, English Desks and Bureaux, English Furniture Designs of the Eighteenth Century, Guide to Osterley Park House, Guide to Ham House, Catalogue of Musical Instruments*, 2 vols, *Musical Instruments as Works of Art*.

Among the many books that touch upon this subject, the following are especially useful and contain illustrations of many pieces of furniture in the Museum collection:

G. Beard. *Georgian Craftsmen and their Work*, 1966.

The Connoisseur Period Guides. *The Early Georgian Period*, 1961, and *The Late Georgian Period*, 1957.

R. Edwards. *The Dictionary of English Furniture*, 3 vols., revised edition, 1954.

R. Edwards. *The Shorter Dictionary of English Furniture*, 1964.

R. Edwards and M. Jourdain. *Georgian Cabinet Makers*, 3rd ed., 1955.

R. Fastnedge. *English Furniture Styles*, Pelican, 1955, and subsequent editions.

R. Fastnedge. *Sheraton Furniture*, 1962.

J. Gloag. *The Englishman's Chair*, 1965.

J. Gloag. *A Social History of Furniture Design*, 1966.

C. Musgrave. *Adam and Hepplewhite Furniture*, 1966.

C. Musgrave. *Regency Furniture*, 1961.

P. Ward-Jackson. 'Some main streams and tributaries in European ornament 1500–1750,' Part 3, in *Victoria and Albert Museum Bulletin*, Vol. 3, no. 4, October, 1967.

A. Coleridge, *Chippendale Furniture*, 1968.

NOTE

The furniture shown in the general views of the period rooms (Figs. 14, 19, 54, 82, 86, 87, 88, 89) has in some cases been moved since these photographs were taken. For further information about these pieces or about any of the furniture illustrated in this book, please apply to the Department of Furniture and Woodwork.

LIST OF PLATES

Frontispiece. BEDSTEAD. Japanned wood, with modern yellow silk curtains. About 1755
W.143-1921

1 CHAIR. Carved beechwood, gessoed and gilded. About 1717
W.62-1935

2 SETTEE. Walnut, upholstered in contemporary Soho tapestry. Early eighteenth century
W.29-1947

3 LONG-CASE CLOCK. Oak case with walnut veneer and marquetry of rosewood, sycamore, pear and walnut. About 1720
W.24-1938

4 LONG-CASE CLOCK. Oak and pine-wood with carved, japanned and silvered decoration. About 1715
W.17-1937

5 BRACKET CLOCK. Wooden case decorated with panels of mirror glass, brass mounts and glass columns. First quarter of the eighteenth century
W.30-1964

6 BRACKET CLOCK. In a case with japanned decoration. About 1730
W.7-1944

7 STOOL. Carved walnut, upholstered in Genoa velvet. About 1720
W.55-1926

8 LIBRARY READING-CHAIR. Carved mahogany, upholstered in leather. About 1720
W.47-1948

9 BUREAU-CABINET. Walnut with inlay of other woods. About 1720
W.66-1924

10 MIRROR. Pinewood frame with burr-walnut veneer and gilt gesso detail. About 1730
W.16-1927

11 CHEST. Carved and gilded gesso on wood. About 1720
W.33-1948

12 TOP OF A SIDE-TABLE. Oak covered with carved and gilded gesso. About 1720
W.94-1962

13 CEILING. Detail of ceiling illustrated in fig. 14
W.5-1960

14 DRAWING ROOM. With fireplace and ceiling from No. 11 Henrietta Place, St. Marylebone. About 1722-25
W.5-1960

15 MIRROR. Pinewood frame, carved and gilded. About 1730
W.44-1927

16 CHAIR. Carved wood, gessoed and gilded, with old upholstery. About 1730
Lent by the Ashmolean Museum

17 CHANDELIER. Carved and gilded wood. About 1730
416-1882

18 HARPSICHORD. Case of walnut.
About 1725
466-1882

19 PANELLED ROOM from No. 26
Hatton Garden, London. Carved
and painted pinewood. About 1730
W.4-1912

20 WALL LANTERN. Carved
mahogany. About 1730
W.63-1950

21 SIDE-TABLE. Carved and gilt
wood, with scagliola top.
About 1726
W.6-1933

22 TABLE TOP. Detail from table
top illustrated in fig. 21

23 SIDE-TABLE. Carved pinewood,
painted white; white marble top.
About 1730
W.3-1953

24 SETTEE. Pinewood, carved,
painted, and gilded; modern
upholstery. About 1735
W.48-1934

25 SETTEE. Carved and gilded
mahogany. Modern upholstery.
About 1740
W.8-1964

26 MIRROR. Frame of carved and
gilded pinewood. About 1740
W.86-1911

27 CONSOLE TABLE. Carved,
gilded and gessoed wood. Top of
green marble. About 1730
W.21-1945

28 PEDESTAL. Carved pine painted
in imitation of mahogany. Second
quarter of the eighteenth century
W.47-1962

29 CHAIR. Carved mahogany,
upholstered in contemporary
needlework. About 1730
Lent by the Leicester Museum and
Art Gallery

30 SIDE-TABLE. Carved mahogany
with gilt enrichments. Second
quarter of the eighteenth century
W.4-1965

31 COMMODE. Carved mahogany.
About 1730
W.57-1962

32 BOOKCASE. Pinewood, carved
and painted with gilded enrichments. About 1730
W.2-1923

33 LIBRARY TABLE. Carved
mahogany. About 1740-50
W.12-1960

34 MEDAL CABINET. Carved
mahogany. About 1750-61
W.11-1963

35 CABINET. Carved mahogany.
About 1740-50
W.75-1962

36 SECRETARY. Mahogany, the
pediment veneered with tortoiseshell, inlay and mounts of brass.
About 1735
W.37-1953

Georgian Furniture

37 CABINET ON STAND. Mahogany, inlaid with engraved brass mounts. About 1735
w.7-1964

38 ARM-CHAIR. Carved rosewood, inlaid with engraved brass, the seat covered with contemporary needlework. About 1735-40
w.32-1959

39 BUREAU DRESSING TABLE. Carved mahogany with gilded bronze mounts. About 1740-50
w.4-1956

40 MIRROR AND SIDE TABLE. Carved wood, bronzed and gilded, the top of the table veneered with onyx. Mid eighteenth century
w.35-1964

41 SIDE-TABLE. Carved walnut with marble top. About 1730-40
w.40-1920

42 SIDE-TABLE. Carved and gilded pine. About 1740
w.3-1961

43 CABINET. Carved rosewood with figures of Palladio, Il Fiammingo and Inigo Jones, the arms of Walpole, eagle heads and seventeenth century Italian plaques of ivory. Made in 1743
w.52-1925

44 LONG-CASE CLOCK. Oak with japanned decoration. About 1750
w.20-1946

45 LONG-CASE CLOCK. Walnut veneer on oak. Second quarter of the eighteenth century
w.107-1962

46 SPINET. Case veneered with burr walnut, boxwood and ebony stringing. Dated 1758
w.43-1922

47 PEDESTAL WRITING-TABLE. Carved mahogany. Dated 1751
w.8-1942

48 ARMILLARY SPHERE. Carved mahogany with celestial sphere in brass. About 1750
w.36-1938

49 READING DESK. Mahogany. Second quarter of the eighteenth century
w.83-1962

50 WASHSTAND. Carved and turned mahogany. About 1760
w.50-1910

51 CLOCK. In a case with japanned decoration. About 1750
w.51-1927

52 MIRROR. Carved and gilded frame. About 1760
w.12-1959

53 WALL LANTERN. Carved mahogany, partly gilded, with glass panels. Mid-eighteenth century
w.26-1954

54 THE MUSIC ROOM from the Norfolk House, St. James's Square, London. Carved pine with plaster decoration. Completed in 1756
w.70-1938

55 ARM-CHAIR. Carved wood and gilded. Second quarter of the eighteenth century
w.36-1964

56 SETTEE. Carved mahogany, upholstered with maroon morocco leather. Mid-eighteenth century
w.6-1965

57 STOOL. Carved mahogany, re-upholstered with contemporary embroidery. About 1755
w.39-1946

58 TABLE. Carved mahogany. Mid-eighteenth century
w.66-1953

59 ARM-CHAIR. Carved mahogany, upholstered with modern velvet. Third quarter of the eighteenth century
w.72-1962

60 ARM-CHAIR. Carved mahogany, with damask upholstery. About 1760
w.47-1946

61 ORGAN-CASE. Carved mahogany. About 1760-65
w.37-1931

62 MANTELPIECE AND MIRROR Carved pine with marble slips. About 1750
738-1897

63 PAIR OF BRACKETS. Carved
a-b and gilded pinewood, the gilding modern. About 1760
w.50 & a-1946

64 CANDLE-STAND. Carved mahogany. Mid-eighteenth century
w.60-1962

65 CANDLE-STAND. Carved pinewood. About 1760
w.9-1950

66 MIRROR. Pinewood frame with carved and gilded gesso decoration. About 1766
2388-1855

67 POLE-SCREEN. Carved mahogany, with petit-point embroidery. About 1760
w.1-1928

68 POLE-SCREEN. Carved mahogany, with contemporary needlework in tent-stitch. Mid-eighteenth century
w.68-1962

69 POLE-SCREEN. Carved mahogany. Third quarter of the eighteenth century
w.34-1959

70 FIRE-SCREEN. Carved mahogany containing a panel of petit-point. About 1755
w.2-1933

71 BAROMETER AND THERMOMETER. Carved mahogany case. About 1755
w.27-1926

72 HANGING CLOCK. Mahogany case with carved and applied gilded decoration. About 1760
w.4-1935

73 TEA-TABLE. Carved mahogany. About 1750
w.34-1938

27 ❧ Georgian Furniture

74 ARM-CHAIR. Carved mahogany, upholstered in needlework. About 1755
w.12-1938

75 CHAIR. Carved mahogany with modern upholstery. About 1765-70
w.9-1932

76 CABINET ON STAND. Carved mahogany, the finials of gilt metal. Mid-eighteenth century
w.65-1953

77 COMMODE. Oak with japanned decoration, brass mounts. About 1765
w.61-1931

78 SETTEE. Carved mahogany; upholstered in Chinese painted satin. Mid-eighteenth century
w.7-1946

79 COMMODE. Japanned wood. About 1753
w.55-1952

80 BREAKFAST-TABLE. Mahogany. About 1755
w.64-1950

81 ARM-CHAIR. Mahogany, upholstered in modern silk. About 1760-70
w.46-1962

82 THE 'STRAWBERRY ROOM' from Lee Priory, Littlebourne, near Canterbury, Kent. Painted pinewood. About 1782-90
w.48-1953

83 KETTLE-STAND. Carved mahogany. Third quarter of the eighteenth century
w.7-1961

84 ARTIST'S TABLE. Carved mahogany. Third quarter of the eighteenth century.
w.31-1912

85 READING-TABLE. Carved mahogany. Made in 1770
w.202-1923

86 THE LIBRARY at Osterley Park House. Dates from 1766

87 THE EATING ROOM at Osterley Park House. Dates from 1767

88 THE TAPESTRY ROOM at Osterley Park House. Dates from 1775

89 DRAWING-ROOM. With fireplace and ceiling from No. 5, the Adelphi Terrace, London. Designed by Robert and James Adam and occupied by David Garrick. About 1770
w.42 & 43-1936

90 ARM-CHAIR. Carved and gilded beechwood, upholstered in crimson silk. About 1764
w.1-1937

91 WALL DECORATION. Detail of wall decoration in the Glass Drawing Room from Northumberland House, London. About 1771
w.3-1955

92 SIDE-BOARD PEDESTAL. Carved mahogany. About 1765
w.38-1934

93 CANDELABRUM AND
    PEDESTAL. (both one of a pair).
    About 1765
    Candelabrum: w.23-1934
    Pedestal: w.24-1934

94 GIRANDOLE. Frame of carved
    and gilded wood. About 1770
    Osterley Park House.

95a CANDLE-STAND. Carved
    mahogany and pine wood, painted
    with the original colours in blue
    and ivory. About 1771
    w.36-1946

95b CANDLE-STAND. Carved and
    gilt wood. About 1770
    w.72-1923

95c CANDLE-STAND. Pinewood,
    carved and gilded. About 1770
    w.37-1937

96 ARM-CHAIR. Carved and gilt
    wood, upholstered in modern silk.
    About 1775
    W.42-1946

97 CABINET. Marquetry of satin-
    wood, rosewood and other woods,
    set with marble intarsia panels,
    and with mounts of gilded brass.
    About 1771
    w.43-1949

98 CARD-TABLE. Carved
    mahogany. About 1765-70
    w.1-1927

99 DRESSING-COMMODE.
    Mahogany, inlaid with satinwood,
    the mouldings ebonized.
    About 1775
    w.55-1937

100 CABINET. Mahogany, inlaid
    with satinwood, About 1775
    w.50-1936

101 ARM-CHAIR. Carved
    mahogany; modern
    upholstery. About 1775
    w.21-1922

102 ARM-CHAIR. Carved
    mahogany, upholstered in modern
    yellow damask. Third quarter
    of the eighteenth century
    w.8-1961

103 COMMODE. Mahogany, with
    marquetry of rosewood, satinwood,
    tulip and holly, ormolu mounts.
    About 1772
    w.30-1937

104 COMMODE. Satinwood with
    laburnum banding and mar-
    quetry of various woods.
    About 1775
    w.88-1924

105 TROPHY. Detail of trophy on
    right-hand door of the commode
    illustrated in fig. 104
    w.88-1924

106 DRESSING-TABLE. Mahogany
a-b overlaid with marquetry of
    satinwood, laburnum and other
    woods. About 1770
    w.89-1924

107 PEDESTAL DRESSING-
    TABLE. Mahogany with king-
    wood veneer and marquetry of
    various woods. About 1775
    w.55-1928

29 ❧ Georgian Furniture

108 COMMODE. Harewood inlaid with satinwood, tulip, burr-walnut and holly. About 1782
w.56-1925

109 LONG-CASE CLOCK. Carved mahogany case with brass face partly silvered. About 1780
w.81-1910

110 LONG-CASE CLOCK. Carved mahogany, with gilded brass mounts. About 1775
w.50-1937

111 DRESSING-TABLE. Mahogany
a-b veneered with harewood. Late eighteenth century
w.14-1959

112 URN-TABLE. Satinwood with painted decoration. Dated 1790
w.45-1935

113 PEMBROKE TABLE. Satinwood with marquetry of various woods. Late eighteenth century
w.6-1959

114 SIDE-TABLE. Pinewood,
a-b painted and gilt. About 1780
349a-1871

115 SIDE-TABLE, of gilt wood with
a-b painted top. About 1793
w.42-1928

116 ARM-CHAIR. Satinwood, painted in polychrome. Made in 1790 by George Seddon.
w.1-1968

117 ARM-CHAIR. Mahogany with painted decoration. Modern upholstery. About 1785
w.52-1946

118 ARM-CHAIR. Carved mahogany with metal details; upholstered in modern silk. About 1775
45-1869

119 ARM-CHAIR. Carved mahogany; modern upholstery. About 1783-90
w.64-1930

120 PAIR OF KNIFE BOXES. Yew
a-b veneer, with silver mounts. About 1770
w.90 & a-1926

121 TEA-CADDIES. Inlaid;
a-c (a) harewood; (b) satinwood; (c) walnut; about 1790
w.98, 108, 101-1919

122 KNIFE-CASE. Satinwood, with painted decoration. About 1780
w.28-1912

123 TERRESTRIAL GLOBE. On mahogany stand, the stand dated about 1800. Globe dated 1843
w.52-1916

124 DRESSING CASE AND STAND. Laburnum or possibly olive wood. Third quarter of the eighteenth century
w.26-1962

125 BAROMETER AND THERMOMETER. Mahogany case, brass mouldings and painted glass. About 1800
w.18-1936

126 SECRETARY-BOOKCASE. Satinwood with inlay of various woods, painted decoration. About 1790
w.121-1924

127 BUREAU-BOOKCASE. Inlaid satinwood. Late eighteenth century
w.84-1910

128 MIRROR. Pinewood frame, carved and gilded with convex glass. About 1800
w.85-1926

129 MIRROR. Carved and gilded pinewood frame. About 1810
w.60-1937

130 LIBRARY STEPS. Mahogany. About 1790
w.7-1932

131 LIBRARY TABLE. Mahogany veneered with sabicu wood. About 1810
w.28-1938

132 SIDEBOARD. Carved mahogany. About 1800
w.41-1950

133 DRESSING-TABLE. Carved mahogany, inlaid with ebony. About 1805
w.25-1946

134 STAND. Carved mahogany. About 1810
w.35-1946

135 LIBRARY TABLE. Rosewood with carved and gilded gesso decoration. About 1810
w.49-1946

136 SETTEE. Carved and gilt beechwood, upholstered in modern silk. Made in 1805
w.38-1930

137 SECRETARY. Mahogany veneered with zebrawood and bands of satinwood. The masks and feet of brass. About 1808
w.15-1930

138 HANGING CABINET. Mahogany inlaid with brass, metal and various woods. About 1810-20
w.63-1935

139 CABINET. Satinwood with inlaid banding, painted detail and gilt brass mounts. About 1820
w.64-1953

140 SECRETARY. Rosewood with satinwood stringing and brass mounts. About 1810
w.10-1944

141 CHAIR. Beech, japanned black and gilded. First quarter of the nineteenth century
w.27-1958

142 TEA POY. Rosewood with marquetry of various woods. (Tunbridge ware). About 1825
w.5-1931

143 PEDESTAL TABLE. Coromandel wood veneer and lacquered brass mounts. Made about 1820
Osterley Park House

144 SIDEBOARD. Rosewood inlaid with brass. About 1820.
w.149-1923

PLATES

1
CHAIR
Carved beechwood, gessoed and
gilded. About 1717. Contemporary
Genoa velvet. Arms, granted in 1717, of
Sir William Humphreys, Bart., Lord
Mayor of London, 1714-15. This chair
is very similar to a set at Houghton,
Norfolk.

Height 121·9cm (4ft)
Width 62·2cm (2ft 0½in)

w.62-1935

2
SETTEE
Walnut. Upholstered in contemporary Soho tapestry. Early eighteenth century. One of a pair (the other now in the National Gallery of Victoria, Melbourne) from a set which included sixteen chairs, from Glemham Hall, Suffolk. They were made for a member of the North family, later Earls of Guilford.

Height 105·9cm (3ft 6 in)
Width 154·9cm (5ft 1in)

W.29-1947

3
LONG-CASE CLOCK
Oak case with walnut veneer and marquetry of rosewood, sycamore, pear and walnut. About 1720. Movement by William Halstead, London. Bequeathed by Mrs A. Anderson.

Height 289·5cm (9ft 7½in)
Width   57·1cm (1ft 10½in)

w.24-1938

4
LONG-CASE CLOCK
Oak and pine-wood with carved,
japanned and silvered decoration.
About 1715. Movement by Thomas
Windmills of St. Martin's-le-Grand.
He became a Member of the Clock-
makers' Company in 1695 and Master
of the Company in 1719.
Hudson Bequest.

Height 266·6cm (8ft 8in)
Width 57·1cm (1ft 10½in)

W.17-1937

5
BRACKET CLOCK
Wooden case decorated with panels of mirror glass, brass mounts and glass columns. First quarter of the eighteenth century. The movement by Joseph Windmills & Son of London. Given by Brigadier W. E. Clark, C.M.G., D.S.O., through the National Art-Collections Fund.

Height   55·9cm (1ft 10in)
Width   43·2cm (1ft 5in)

W.30-1964

6

BRACKET CLOCK
In a case with japanned decoration.
About 1730. By James Markwick, the
younger; Member of the Clockmakers'
Company in 1692 and Master in 1720.
Johnson Bequest.

Height 45·7cm (1ft 6in)
Width 26·6cm (10½ in)

W.7-1944

7
STOOL
Carved walnut, upholstered
in Genoa velvet. About 1720. One of
a pair. Croft Lyons Bequest.

Height 48·3cm (1ft 7in)
Width 50·8cm (1ft 8in)

W.55-1926

LIBRARY READING-CHAIR
About 1720. Carved mahogany upholstered in leather. In the arms are swivel drawers for writing equipment. Thought to have been in the possession of the poet John Gay (1685-1732). The reader would sit facing the back, his legs astride with a book open on the desk. They are sometimes called cock-fighting chairs, but this is not a contemporary term. This type of chair was still manufactured almost a century later, for Thomas Sheraton in *The Cabinet Directory* (1803) illustrates one on plate 41 and mentions in the text that the chair was intended 'to make the exercise [of reading] easy, and for the convenience of taking down a note or quotation from any subject'.

Height 83·9cm (2ft 9in)
Width 78·8cm (2ft 7in)

W.47-1948

9

BUREAU-CABINET
Walnut with inlay of other woods.
About 1720. On the inside of the door
is inlaid the inscription *Samuel
Bennett London Fecit*. Bennett had
his workshop in Monmouth Square.
Given by the National Art-Collections
Fund.

Height 274·3cm (9ft 0½in)
Width   95·8cm (3ft 2in)

w.66-1924

10
MIRROR
Pinewood frame with burr-walnut veneer and gilt gesso detail. About 1730.

Height 114·3cm (3ft 9in)
Width 68cm (2ft 2¾in)

W.16-1927

11
CHEST
Carved and gilded gesso on wood. About 1720. From Shobden Court, Hertfordshire. Bears the monogram of William Bateman, created Viscount Bateman in 1725. Bateman was a great traveller and would certainly have noted the many chests (*cassoni*) that were to be found in the Renaissance palaces of Italy. This may have encouraged him to acquire this chest, which shows the influence of the designs for sarcophagi engraved by Jean Berain. Berain was an important source of the early Georgian style and William Kent was much influenced by his ornamental designs. The chest and coffer had been used for storage purposes since the Middle Ages, but by the early eighteenth century the form was mostly used as an ornamental feature in the splendid state rooms of the newly fashionable Palladian houses. In the second quarter of the century they were replaced by the more practical chest-of-drawers for, as the French name for this article shows, it was 'plus commode'. Compare with fig. 31.

Height   78·8cm (2ft 7in)
Width   144·8cm (4ft 9in)

W.33-1948

12

THE TOP OF A SIDE-TABLE
Oak, covered with carved and gilded gesso. About 1720. From Glemham Hall, Suffolk, the seat of the North family, Earls of Guilford. This table has a gilded stand of a somewhat later date. Rotch Bequest.

Diameter 62·2cm (2ft 0½in)
Width   111·1cm (3ft 8in)

w.94-1962

13
CEILING
Detail of the ceiling from No. 11 Henrietta Place, St. Marylebone, illustrated in Fig. 14.

w.5-1960

DRAWING-ROOM
With fireplace and ceiling from No. 11 Henrietta Place, St. Marylebone. Henrietta Place formed part of a terrace designed by James Gibbs and built between about 1722-25. No. 11 was let to Gibbs himself although he did not occupy it. The arms on the overmantel are those of the Allen family, who occupied the house during the third quarter of the eighteenth century. It was demolished in 1956.

The design for the door and window dressings are close to a design in Gibbs's *Book of Architecture* (London, 1728). The plasterwork of the ceiling was probably executed by G. Artari and G. Bagutti, who did similar work for Gibbs at Ditchley and at St. Peter's Church, almost opposite the house in Henrietta Place, at this time. The ceiling paintings are attributed to Antonio Belluci of Treviso, then working in England. They represent Apollo, Time unveiling Truth and Love repelling Hatred and four grisailles emblematic of the Arts. The material on the walls and parquet floor are modern.

w.5-1960

FURNITURE IN THE GIBBS ROOM
Left
CARD TABLE. Parquetry of laburnum. About 1715. Given by Mr Eric M. Browett.
w.51-1937

BRACKET CLOCK. Ebony veneer on oak. About 1700. The brass dial inscribed *John Knibb/Oxon*. Bequeathed by Mrs Gertrude M. Winstanley.
w.24-1946

GO-CART. Turned ash and mahogany. First quarter of the eighteenth century. Given by Mr B. Middleton.
w.36-1937

POLE-SCREEN. Tapestry panel of silk and wools. Mid-eighteenth century. The stand is of later date. Croft Lyons Bequest.
w.59-1926

LONG-CASE CLOCK. Figured walnut. About 1730. The brass dial inscribed *Benjamin Gray and Justin Vulliamy London*. Given by Mr S. E. Prestidge.
w.65-1929

Centre:
SETTEE AND PAIR OF CHAIRS. Walnut veneer. About 1725.
676, 678 & 680-1890

CARD TABLE. Oak veneered with walnut, the legs of carved walnut. About 1725.
223-1904

Right:
CARD TABLE. Walnut veneered with burr walnut and figured walnut. About 1725. Given by Mrs Bomer.
w.22-1929

15
MIRROR
Pinewood frame, carved and gilded. About 1730. Incorporating a barometer and thermometer and bracket for a clock.

Height 227·2cm (7ft 5½in)
Width   66·1cm (2ft 2in)

W.44-1927

16
CHAIR
Carved wood, gessoed and gilded, with old upholstery. About 1730. One of the most magnificent chairs of its date and related in style to examples at the Lady Lever Art Gallery, Port Sunlight, and at Beningborough, Yorkshire. Lent by the Ashmolean Museum.

Height 112·9cm (3ft 6in)
Width   64·4cm (2ft)

17
CHANDELIER
Carved and gilded wood. About 1730.
The strong French character of this
piece suggests that the designer was
conversant with the engraved composi-
tions of such French artists as Berain,
Le Pautre and Marot in England.
From Hamilton Palace, Fife.

Height 98·4cm (3ft 3in)

416-1882

18

HARPSICORD

Case of walnut. About 1725. Above the keyboards is the inscription *Thomas Hitchcock, Londini, Fecit*. Elaborate keyboards such as this were a speciality of the Hitchcock family. The harpsicord came from Ightham Mote, Kent. Given by Mrs Luard-Selby.

Height 26cm (10½in)
Length 233cm (7ft 10in)

466-1882

19
PANELLED ROOM
Carved and painted pine wood. From
No. 26 Hatton Garden, London.
About 1730. Given by the National
Art-Collections Fund and a body of
subscribers.

W.4-1912

FURNITURE IN THE HATTON
GARDEN ROOM
Left to Right.

HALL ARM-CHAIR. Carved mahogany.
About 1730. Given by Mr F. H. Reed.
W.63-1953

ARMILLARY SPHERE. (See Fig. 48).
W.36-1953

LIBRARY ARM-CHAIR. Carved
mahogany, parcel gilt; covered with
leather. About 1730. Lent by
Miss Louise W. Stone.

LIBRARY DESK. Carved mahogany.
About 1755-60.
W.56-1948

CHAIR (at back). Walnut. Early
eighteenth century.
235-1898

TEA-KETTLE STAND. Carved
mahogany. About 1755. Given by
Mr Eric M. Browett.
W.52-1937

ARM-CHAIR (in front). Walnut. About
1720. Given by the children of the late
Sir George Donaldson.
W.38-1925

COMMODE. Carved mahogany. About
1740. Attributed to William Vile,
cabinet-maker to George III.
Rotch Bequest.
W.74-1962

CARD-TABLE. Mahogany. About
1740-50. Croft Lyons Bequest.
W.53-1926

ARM-CHAIR. Carved mahogany.
Second quarter of the eighteenth
century. Lent by the Duke of Buccleuch,
K.T., G.C.V.O.

BAROMETER. Walnut veneer on oak.
Second quarter of the eighteenth
century. Inscribed *J. Hallifax Barnsley
Invt et Fecit*. John Hallifax of Barnsley
lived from 1694 till 1750. Given by
Brigadier W. E. Clark, C.M.G., D.S.O.,
through the National Art-Collections
Fund.
W.10-1960

CHANDELIER. (See Fig. 17.)
416-1882.

WALL LANTERN
Carved mahogany. About 1730. One
of a pair. Given by Brigadier
W. E. Clark, C.M.G., D.S.O.

Height 3cm (2ft 8in)
Width 40·7cm (1ft 4in)

w.63-1950

21
SIDE-TABLE
Carved and gilt wood. Scagliola top bearing the arms of the second Earl of Litchfield. About 1726. Concerning the top of this table Admiral Fitzroy Lee wrote to his brother Litchfield at Ditchley from Leghorn on 26th July 1726: 'I have seen this morning your table which is entirely finished only the arms and supporters which I writ to you of ten months ago, and you have not sent them yet, which is a great pity, for I'm sure it will be the finest of the sort in Europe!' The stand, which has been often attributed, with no evidence, to Henry Flitcroft owing to the fact that he was working at Ditchley, has been shortened to fit the top. Scagliola, a plaster of pulverized selenite had been used in Italy since classical times. The technique was perfected by Enrico Hugford and his school in Florence between 1737 and 1771.

Height 83·9cm (2ft 9in)
Width 145·4cm (4ft 9¼in)

w.6-1933

22
TABLE TOP
Detail from the table top illustrated in fig. 21.

w.6-1933

23
SIDE-TABLE
Carved pinewood painted white, white marble top. About 1730. From Coleshill House, Berkshire. A similar table is at Longford Castle, Wiltshire. This is a particularly felicitous example of the kind of 'state-room' furniture made under the influence of William Kent for the embellishment of the formal, temple-like interiors of English Palladian houses.
Given by Mr E. E. Cook.

Height   92·9cm (3ft $\frac{3}{4}$in)
Width   198·1cm (6ft 6in)

W.3-1953

24
SETTEE
Softwood, carved, painted and gilded; modern upholstery. About 1735. In the style of William Kent and closely resembling a settee at Holkham, which was probably designed under his directions.

Height 99·6cm (3ft 3½in)
Width 167·6cm (5ft 6in)

W.48-1934

25
SETTEE
Carved and gilded mahogany. Modern
upholstery. About 1740. In the style
of William Kent and similar to the seat
furniture at Holkham. From Wroxton
Abbey, Oxfordshire and part of a set of
ten chairs and two settees, made for
Francis North, first Earl of Guilford.
While the carving of this settee is of
the highest quality, the design consists
of a somewhat disjointed assembly
of Kentian forms.

Height 100·8cm (3ft 4in)
Width 210·8cm (6ft 11½in)

w.8-1964

26
MIRROR
Frame of carved and gilded pinewood. About 1740. Perhaps made for Frederick, Prince of Wales—hence the feathers—and probably designed by William Kent as it closely relates to the design for the stern of the Prince of Wales's Barge. See John Vardy, *Some Designs of Mr. Inigo Jones and of Mr. William Kent* (London, 1744), pl. 52. It may have been made by Benjamin Goodison, who is known to have supplied furniture for the Royal Household at this period. He was also responsible for making the Barge. Gift of Sir Edward Stern.

Height 179cm (5ft 10½in)
Width 69·2cm (2ft 5¼in)

w.86-1911

27
CONSOLE TABLE
Carved, gilded and gessoed wood.
About 1730. In the style of William
Kent. Top of green marble (*verde
antique*).

Height 90·1cm (2ft 11½in)
Width 98·4cm (3ft 3in)

W.21-1945

PEDESTAL
Carved pine painted in imitation of
mahogany. Second quarter of the
eighteenth century. One of a pair.
Similar examples at Chatsworth and
Hampton Court are probably
attributable to Benjamin Goodison
under the influence of William Kent,
although a drawing by John Vardy
exists for a very similar pedestal. See
Peter Ward-Jackson, *English Furniture
Designs of the Eighteenth Century* (London,
1958) pl. 41 and pl. 37. Pedestals very
closely duplicating the Vardy design
are at Longford Castle, Wiltshire.

Height 127cm (4ft 2in)
Width   32cm (1ft 0¾in)

W.47-1962

29
CHAIR
Carved mahogany; upholstered in contemporary needlework. About 1730. This piece exemplifies the way in which mahogany – which, at this time, had only recently come into fashion for furniture – lent itself to intricate carving in a style quite different from that which was possible when walnut was the principal material. Lent by the Leicester Museum and Art Gallery.

Height 107·9cm (3ft 6¾in)
Width 65·4cm (2ft 1¾in)

30
SIDE-TABLE
Carved mahogany with gilt enrichments.
Second quarter of the eighteenth
century. Shows the influence of William
Kent. A similar table is at Alnwick
Castle, Northumberland.

Height 88·9cm (2ft 11in)
Width 123·1cm (4ft 0½in)

W.4-1965

31
COMMODE
Carved mahogany. About 1730. This piece presents furniture historians with something of a puzzle. It may be an early English attempt to imitate a French *bombé* chest of drawers or commode. Alternatively, it may be of Dutch origin, in which case it should date from the middle of the century. Compare with the Bateman chest shown in Fig. 11.

Height 90·8cm (2ft 11¾in)
Width 141·6cm (4ft 7in)

W.57-1962

32
BOOKCASE
Pinewood, carved and painted with gilded enrichments. About 1730. Style of William Kent. The lower section has been reduced in height, probably by about 30cm (12in).

Height 215·9cm (7ft 1½in)
Width 170·2cm (5ft 7in)

W.2-1923

33
LIBRARY TABLE
Carved mahogany. About 1740-50.
The rectangular top is divided into
two halves. One can be raised and
tilted in either position by a ratchet and
spring system. There are two concealed
bookrests and the front of the table can
be unlocked and pulled forward to
reveal a writing desk. Attributed to
William Vile, the Royal cabinet-maker,
and similar to a pair of commodes at
Goodwood, Sussex and another pair
at Alnwick, Northumberland. From
Ashburnham Place, Sussex.

Height   91·4cm (3ft)
Width   152·4cm (5ft)

W.12-1960

34

MEDAL CABINET

Carved mahogany. Between about 1750 and 1761. One of a pair (the other now in the Metropolitan Museum, New York) from Stratfield Saye. Believed to have been made either for George III or his father and subsequently acquired by the 2nd Duke of Wellington. They can be identified with entries in the Royal accounts for 1760-61 recording bills from William Vile for alterations to 'His Majesty's Grand Medal Case', which was apparently divided into separate sections of which they both formed two units, see Derek Shrub 'The Vile Problem', *Victoria and Albert Museum Bulletin* (Vol. 1, no. 4, October, 1965) where it is suggested that Vile's partner John Bradburn executed most of the carving, and the cabinet is compared to a four-sided clock carved by Bradburn at Buckingham Palace.

Height 200·6cm (6ft 7in)
Width 69·8cm (2ft 3½in)

W.11-1963

35
CABINET
Carved mahogany. In the style associated with William Vile. About 1740-50. Rotch Bequest.

Height 237·4cm (7ft 9½in)
Width 132·1cm (4ft 4in)

w.75-1962

36

SECRETARY

Mahogany, the pediment veneered with tortoiseshell, mounts of inlay and brass. About 1735. Attributed to the workshop of John Channon. (See figs. 37, 38 and 39).

Height 246·4cm (8ft 3in)
Width   93·3cm (3ft 1in)

W.37-1953

37
CABINET ON STAND

Mahogany, inlaid with engraved brass, and with gilded brass mounts. About 1735. This and figs. 36, 38 and 39 have been attributed to the workshop of John Channon, an important London cabinet maker with premises in St. Martin's Lane. (See John Hayward 'English Brass Inlaid Furniture' *Victoria and Albert Museum Bulletin*, Vol. 1, no. 1, January, 1965, and his 'The Channon Family of Exeter and London, Chair and Cabinet Makers', *Ibid.*, Vol. 2, no. 2, April, 1966). It has been suggested that the German cabinet maker Abraham Roentgen, who worked in London at this period, and specialized in engraved metal inlay-work, may have collaborated with Channon on this cabinet and the related pieces (see figs. above). For Roentgen's English career and his possible connections with Channon, see Peter Thornton and Desmond Fitz-Gerald, 'Abraham Roentgen 'englische Kabinettmacher . . .', *Victoria and Albert Museum Bulletin*, Vol. 2, no. 4, October, 1966.

Height 233·6cm (7ft 8in)
Width   132·7cm (4ft 4½in)

w.7-1964

38
ARM-CHAIR
Carved rosewood, inlaid with engraved brass; the seat covered with contemporary needlework. About 1735-40. The oval escutcheon that centres the inlaid brass decoration engraved with the owner's crest. Brass inlaid furniture such as this has recently been associated with the workshop of John Channon. Second quarter of the eighteenth century. See John Hayward 'English Brass Inlaid Furniture' *Victoria and Albert Museum Bulletin*, Vol. 1, no. 1, January, 1965 (See also figs. 36, 37 and 39). Given by Brigadier W. E. Clark, C.M.G., D.S.O., through the National Art-Collections Fund.

Height 91·4cm (3ft)
Width 53·4cm (1ft 9in)

W.32-1959

39
BUREAU DRESSING TABLE

Carved mahogany with gilded bronze mounts. About 1740-50. The top drawer which extends across the whole piece, is a writing drawer, and is supported on the corner trusses when pulled out. This piece shows considerable Germanic influence and probably originates from the workshop of John Channon (see figs. 36, 37 and 38). The companion half of the desk, which could have been joined to it, back-to-back or with a leaf between, was in the London art market in 1965. Purchased with the aid of a grant from the National Art-Collections Fund and a contribution from Messrs H. Blairman & Sons.

Height 88·9cm (2ft 11in)
Width 157·5cm (5ft 2in)

w.4-1956

40

MIRROR AND SIDE TABLE

Carved wood, bronzed and gilded, the top of the table veneered with onyx. Mid-eighteenth century. From the Tapestry Room at Hinton House, Somerset, and designed by Mathias Lock for the second Earl Poulett. The original sketch by Lock for the table and other furniture designs by him are in the Museum (Department of Prints and Drawings, nos. 2848, 1–168) and it shows that it took eighty-nine days to make, costing £22 5s 5d for the joiner and £21 for the carving. Lock worked on it for fifteen days, the remainder being done by his assistants. The design for the mirror shows that it took one hundred and thirty-eight days work and cost £36 5s, Lock working on it for twenty days. Lock was an exceptionally capable draughtsman who understood the Rococo idiom more fully than any other English furniture designer. See John Hayward 'Furniture designed and carved by Mathias Lock . . .' *Connoisseur*, Vol. CXLVI, December, 1960, p. 284.

Mirror Height 259cm (8ft 7in)
Width 127cm (4ft 2in)

W.8-1960

Table Height 85·1cm (2ft 9½in)
Width 130·6cm (4ft 3½in)

W.35-1964

41
SIDE-TABLE
Carved walnut with marble top.
About 1730-40. Most tables of this
date were carved in mahogany which
afforded a crisper finish.

Height 80·3cm (2ft 7⅝in)
Width 128·2cm (4ft 2⅝in)

W.40-1920

42
SIDE-TABLE
Carved and gilded pine. About 1740.
The travertine top is a replacement.
The design of this table originates from
an engraved plate by Nicholas Pineau
in his *Nouveaux Desseins de Pieds de
Tables* which was plagiarised by
Batty and Thomas Langley in their
*City and County Builder's and Workman's
Treasury of Designs* (1740). Pineau,
with Meissonnier and de la Joue, was
one of the chief originators of the *genre
pittoresque*, as the beginning of the
French Rococo style was termed by
J. F. Blondel. This was soon taken up
in England, as is shown here, although
this table still retains the symmetry
still prevalent in the late Louis XIV
period.

Height 87·6cm (2ft 10½in)
Width 179·2cm (5ft 10½in)

w.3-1961

43
CABINET
Carved rosewood with figures of
Palladio, Il Fiammingo and Inigo
Jones, the arms of Walpole, eagle
heads and seventeenth century Italian
plaques of ivory. Made for Horace
Walpole in 1743. The ivory figures on
the pediment are after Rysbrack and
were carved by Jacob Frans Vescovers
(or Verskovis). Horace Walpole wrote
to Horace Mann in Florence on
July 19th 1743: 'I have a new cabinet
for my enamels and miniatures, just
come home, which I am sure you
would like; it is of rosewood, the door
inlaid with carvings in ivory. I wish
you could see it!' It was later hung
in the Tribune at Strawberry Hill.

Height 152·4cm (5ft)
Width 91·4cm (3ft)

W.52-1925

44
LONG-CASE CLOCK
Oak with japanned decorations.
About 1750. Movement by John
Ellicott of Sweetings Alley, Cornhill.
The hood originally probably had
finials. Winstanley Bequest.

Height 220·9cm (7ft 3in)
Width   50·8cm (1ft 8in)

w.20-1946

45
LONG-CASE CLOCK
Walnut veneer on oak. Second quarter
of the eighteenth century. Movement
by John Ellicott. Rotch Bequest.

Height 251·4cm (8ft 4in)
Width   57·8cm (1ft 10¾in)

W.107-1962

46
SPINET
Case veneered with burr walnut, boxwood and ebony stringing. Signed above the keyboard *Crang Londini fecit* above which is the motto *Musica Laborum Dulce Levamen* and the date 1758. John Crang was one of the best known eighteenth century makers of keyboard instruments in London and it is interesting to note that musical instrument makers continued to use walnut long after it was totally out of fashion in other types of furniture. An old playing card was discovered glued inside, on which the following message was written:
Mrs Weston desires [Mr]
Crang will call to[morrow]
by eleven o'clock [without]
fail the Spinet [is]
so bad she can't [play]
upon it   Tues[day]
Bequeathed by Miss C. A. R. Adams.

Height   25cm ($9\frac{7}{8}$in)
Length 203cm (6ft 8in)

W.43-1922

47
PEDESTAL WRITING-TABLE
Carved mahogany. The second drawer from the bottom on the right is inscribed in ink: *David Wright Fecit Lancaster August 17th 1751*.
Lancaster became a centre of furniture making during the eighteenth century; and the local firm of Gillow was to become famous during the second half of the century.

Height 77·4cm (2ft 6½in)
Width 112·3cm (3ft 8½in)

w.8-1942

48
ARMILLARY SPHERE
Carved mahogany with celestial
sphere in brass. About 1750. Percival
Griffiths Collection. Given by the
National Art-Collections Fund.

Height 97·1cm (3ft 2⅛in)
Diameter 53·4cm (1ft 9in)

w.36-1938

49
READING DESK
Mahogany. Second quarter of the
eighteenth century. The handle
adjusts the main support of the desk
itself which can be raised or lowered.
Rotch Bequest.

Height 114·3cm (3ft 9in)
Width   61cm (2ft)

w.83-1962

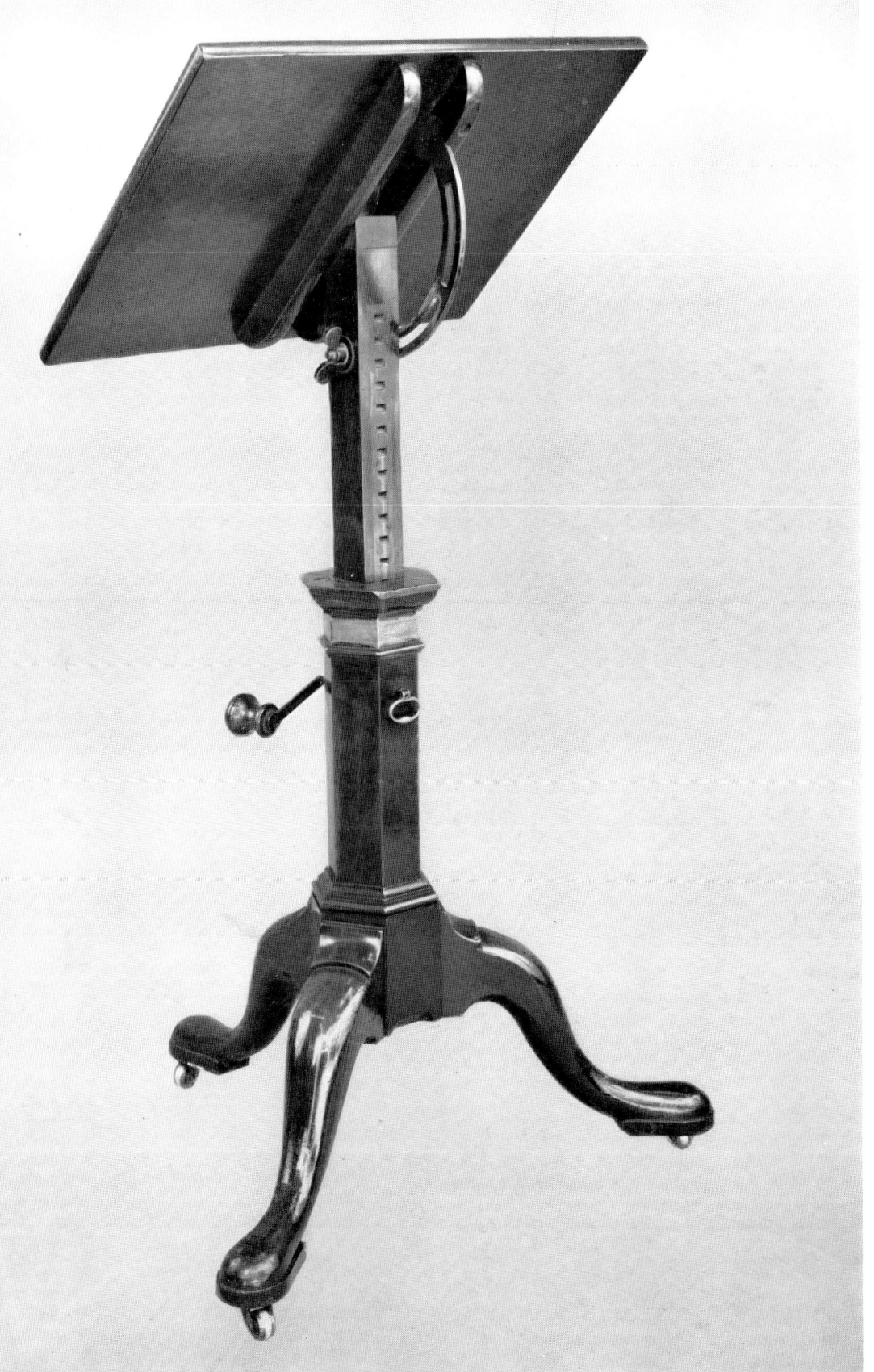

50
WASHSTAND
Carved and turned mahogany. About 1760. The basin and jug are not in place.

Height 81·3cm (2ft 8in)
Width 41·9cm (1ft 4½in)

W.50-1910

51
CLOCK
'Act-of-Parliament' clock in a case with japanned decoration. Inscribed *Humphrey Sellon, Southwark*. About 1750. Mural time pieces such as this were frequently found in public houses and inns, hence the decoration, and are often called 'Act-of-Parliament' clocks, although this is a misnomer, for the Act of Parliament which imposed a tax varying from 2*s* 6*d* to 10*s* upon 'every clock or timekeeper' was not brought in until 1797, at least thirty years after this clock was made.

Height 162·6cm (5ft 4in)
Width   78·8cm (2ft 7in)

W.51-1927

52

MIRROR

Carved and gilded frame. About 1760.
The design closely resembles that of a
pair now in the State Dining Room at
Woburn Abbey, and believed to have
been delivered by the firm of Samuel
and William Norman in 1760. The
Woburn mirrors cost £412.

Height 231·1cm (7ft 7in)
Width   95·8cm (3ft 2in)

W.12-1959

53
WALL LANTERN
Carved mahogany, partly gilded and with glass panels. Mid-eighteenth century. One of a pair. Given by Brigadier W. E. Clark, C.M.G., D.S.O.

Height 62·2cm (2ft 0½in)
Width 56·5cm (1ft 10¼in)

W.26-1954

THE MUSIC ROOM

From the Norfolk House, St. James's Square, London. The house was designed by Matthew Brettingham and completed by 1756. Although the general shape of the room and the design of the Inigo Jones Whitehall-type ceiling are no doubt due to Brettingham, it has been suggested (see Desmond Fitz-Gerald. 'The Norfolk House Music Room', *Victoria and Albert Museum Bulletin*, Vol. 2, no. 1, January, 1966) that the carved pine *Régence* panelling was probably imported from France and partially made up to match in England. The plaster cartouches and trophies are attributed to the sculptor-plasterer William Collins, while the Inigo Jones-style modillion cornice and Whitehall 'frame' are probably by Thomas Clark, who was master plasterer to the Office of Works from 1761-82, and who had worked under Brettingham at Holkham. Given by the Duke of Norfolk, K.G., G.C.V.O., in conjunction with the Norfolk House, St. James's Square Syndicate Ltd, on the demolition of the house in 1938.

W.70-1938

FURNITURE IN THE NORFOLK HOUSE MUSIC ROOM

Left:
PAIR OF ARM-CHAIRS. (See fig. 55)
W.36 & a-1964

BUREAU DRESSING-TABLE. (See fig. 39)
W.4-1956

SETTEE. Gilded pine. About 1740. One of a pair. From Ham House.

Centre:
ARM-CHAIR. Carved mahogany. Mid-eighteenth century. Originally one of a set of six. Given by Brigadier W. E. Clark, C.M.G., D.S.O., through the National Art-Collections Fund.
W.16-1956

STOOL. Carved mahogany, en suite with the arm-chair (see fig. 57)
W.39-1946

TABLE. (See fig. 58)
W.66-1953

Right:
STAND (in corner). Carved and gilt wood. About 1715. In the style of James Moore.
W.1-1952

SIDE-TABLE. (See fig. 42)
W.3-1961

ARM-CHAIR. (See fig. 60)
W.47-1946

55
ARM-CHAIR
Carved wood and gilded. Second quarter of the eighteenth century. One of a pair. The tapestry, which is contemporary, appears to have been added later. From Wentworth Castle, Yorkshire.

Height 103·5cm (3ft 5in)
Width 73·1cm (2ft 4¾in)

w.36-1964

56
SETTEE

Carved mahogany, upholstered with maroon morocco leather. Mid-eighteenth century. The back closely resembles that of a design for a chair by Thomas Chippendale in his *Director* (1st edition, 1754, pl. XVI) and is of a type described by him (*Ibid.*, pl. IX) as a 'Chair with Ribband-Back.' Bequeathed by Mrs M. L. C. Money.

Height 100·2cm (3ft 3¾in)
Width   127cm (4ft 2in)

w.6-1965

57
STOOL
Carved mahogany, re-upholstered with contemporary embroidery. About 1755. The dolphin legs correspond with the front legs of some 'French chairs' in Thomas Chippendale's *Director*, (1st edition, 1754, pl. XX (2)). Another chair in the Museum (W.16-1956) is *ensuite* (see in fig. 54).

Height 46·9cm (1ft 6½in)
Width 64·7cm (2ft 1½in)

W.39-1946

58
TABLE
Carved mahogany. Mid-eighteenth century. The top has possibly been altered. Given by Mr F. H. Reed.

Height 74·9cm (2ft 5½in)

w.66-1953

59
ARM-CHAIR
Carved mahogany, upholstered with modern velvet. Third quarter of the eighteenth century. Reminiscent of Thomas Chippendale's 'French Chairs' in his *Director* (3rd edition, 1762 pls. XX-XXIII).

Height 104·1cm (3ft 5¼in)
Width   72·4cm (2ft 4½in)

W.72-1962

60

ARM-CHAIR

Carved mahogany, with damask upholstery. About 1760-65. Closely corresponds to a design for a 'French Chair' dated 1759, published in Thomas Chippendale's *Director* (3rd edition, 1762 pl. XXIII, right). Said to have come from Gilston Park, Hertfordshire. Given by Brigadier W. E. Clark, C.M.G., D.S.O., through the National Art-Collections Fund.

Height 107·2cm (3ft 6½in)
Width   73·7cm (2ft 5in)

W.47-1946

61
ORGAN-CASE
Carved mahogany. About 1760-65.
Based on a design dated 1760 in
Thomas Chippendale's *Director* (3rd
edition, 1762, pl. IV). The case is
fitted with a keyboard signed *Lincoln
1794*. From Polebarn House,
Trowbridge, Wiltshire.
Bequeathed by Mr J. M. Courage.

Height 350·3cm (11ft 4in)
Width 198·1cm (6ft 6in)

W.37-1931

CHIMNEY-PIECE AND MIRROR
Carved and painted pine with marble slips. From Winchester House, Putney. This admirably reflects the type of English Rococo decoration made popular by Isaac Ware and other members of the so-called Slaughter's Coffee-house set, which included Hogarth, Roubiliac, Gravelot and Hayman, and to a lesser extent Sir Henry Cheere during the 1740's. Ware had published the Rococo interior of Chesterfield House in his *Book of Architecture* in 1756, and had also designed extravagant Rococo work at Woodcote Park. This chimney-piece in wood approximates to Cheere's work in marble at Woodcote (now in the Boston Museum, U.S.A.). About 1750.

Height 320cm (10ft 6¾in)
Width 195·6cm (6ft 5in)

738-1897

63a & b

PAIR OF BRACKETS
Carved and gilded pinewood (gilding modern). About 1760. From the ballroom at Langley Park, Norfolk. The mask of Bacchus corresponds closely with a design dated 1760 in Thomas Chippendale's *Director* (3rd edition, 1762, p. CLXI) entitled 'Brackets for Bustos'.

Height 66·1cm (2ft 2in)
Width 52·7cm (1ft 8¾in)

W.50 & A-1946

64

CANDLE-STAND

Carved mahogany. One of a pair. The gallery is a modern replacement. Mid-eighteenth century. Both are strongly influenced by examples in Thomas Chippendale's *Director* (3rd edition, 1762, pl. CXLV).

Height 140·3cm (4ft 7¼in)

W.60-1962

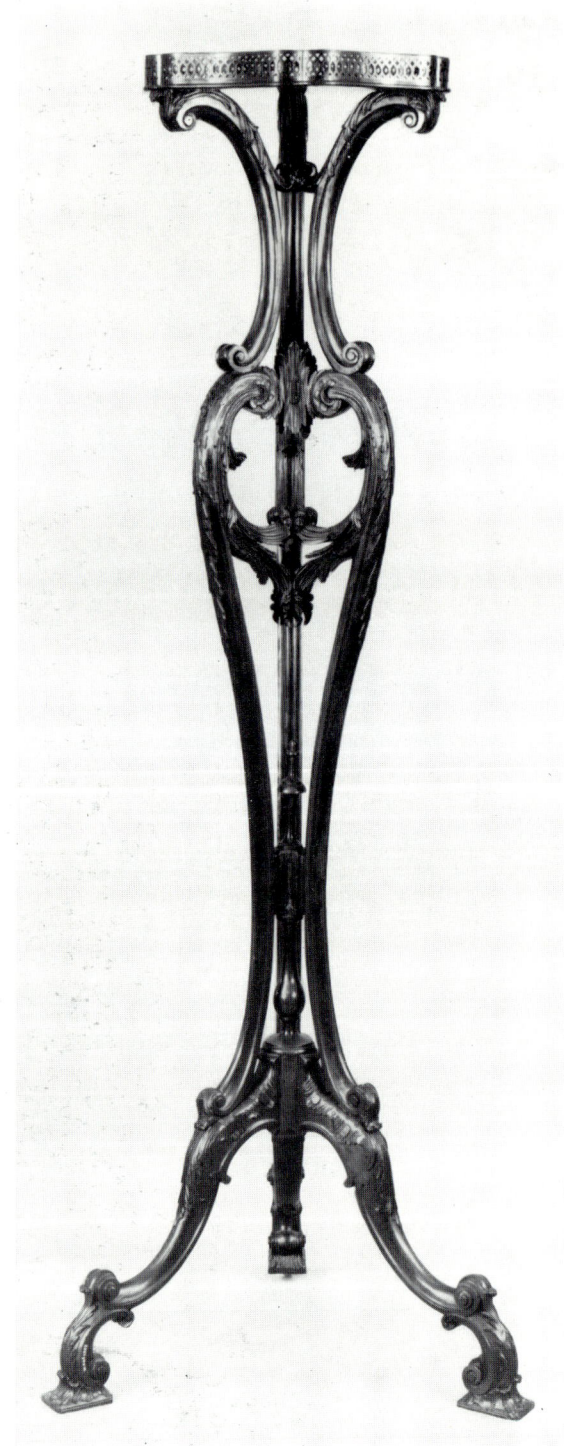

5

CANDLE-STAND
Carved pine partly stained in imitation of mahogany. About 1758. One of a set of four, formerly at Hagley Park, Worcestershire. This closely corresponds to a design, dated 1756, by Thomas Johnson in *One Hundred and Fifty New Designs* (1758), pl. 13c, and adapted by Thomas Chippendale in the *Director* (third edition, 1762 pl. CXLV).
George Lyttelton, 1st Lord Lyttelton, was secretary to Frederick, Prince of Wales; they both eagerly patronised the artists and important craftsmen who belonged to the Rococo-loving Slaughter's Coffee-house set. Lyttelton rebuilt Hagley with elaborate Rococo interiors after his father died in 1751.

Height 158·2cm (5ft 2½in)
Width   55·9cm (1ft 10in)

W.9-1950

66

MIRROR

Pinewood frame with carved and gilded gesso decoration. Probably designed by Thomas Chippendale and possibly one of the two mirrors supplied on the 28th October 1766 to the Duke of Portland: 'To two very large carved frames Gilt in burnished Gold, with three branches for candles to each and brass pans, Noselles to Ditto'. From the Bernal Collection.

Height 213·4cm (7ft)
Width 137·1cm (4ft 6in)

2388-1855

67
POLE-SCREEN
Carved mahogany, with petit-point embroidery. About 1760. Pole-screens of similar type are shown in Thomas Chippendale's *Director* (3rd edition, 1762) and also in William Ince and John Mayhew's *Universal System* (1762-63).

Height 185·1cm (6ft 0½in)
Width 66·1cm (2ft 2in)

W.1-1928

68
POLE-SCREEN
Carved mahogany, with contemporary needlework in tent-stitch.
Mid-eighteenth century.
Rotch Bequest.

Height 170·2cm (5ft 7in)
Width 54·6cm (1ft 9½in)

W.68-1962

69
POLE-SCREEN
Carved mahogany. Third quarter of the eighteenth century. The screen consists of a water-colour apparently of a later date and the stand is close to a design in Thomas Chippendale's *Director* (3rd edition, 1762, pl. CLVI, left). Given by Brigadier W. E. Clark, C.M.G., D.S.O., through the National Art-Collections Fund.

Height 91·4cm (3ft)
Width 38·1cm (1ft 3in)

W.34-1959

70
FIRE-SCREEN
Carved mahogany containing a panel of petit-point. About 1755. The design is based on a plate in Thomas Chippendale's *Director* (1st edition, 1754, pl. CXXVII) with the comment that screens 'standing on four feet are commonly called "Horse-Fire-Screens"'.

Height 95·8cm (3ft 2in)
Width   61cm (2ft)

W.2-1933

71

BAROMETER AND THERMOMETER
Carved mahogany case. About 1755.
Instruments by James Ayscough 'at
the Great Golden Spectacles', Ludgate
Street. Given by Sir Buckston Browne.

Height 105·9cm (3ft 6in)
Width   26·6cm (10½in)

W.27-1926

72

HANGING CLOCK
Mahogany case with carved and
applied gilded decoration. About 1760.
A more sophisticated version of
fig. 51. Given by Lord Riddell.

Height 177·8cm (5ft 10in)
Width 73·1cm (2ft 4¾in)

W.4-1935

73
TEA-TABLE
Carved mahogany. About 1750. This shows a very late use of the ball and claw foot.

Height 72·4cm (2ft 4½in)
Width 80cm (2ft 7½in)

W.34-1938

74

ARM-CHAIR

Carved mahogany, upholstered in
needlework. About 1755. One of a pair,
numbered II and X and originally
from a large set, the settee of which is
in the Werner Collection at Luton Hoo.
They are particularly stylish and
opulent examples of the Chippendale
manner. Cross-stretchers, such as appear
on these chairs, are unusual at this
date.
Given by Lady Theobald.

Height 101·6cm (3ft 4½in)
Width   76·8cm (2ft 6¼in)

W.12-1938

75
CHAIR
Carved mahogany, with modern upholstery. About 1765-70. One of a pair. Though these chairs are often called 'in the style of Robert Manwairing' they are in fact far closer to designs by Matthew Darly in his *New Book of Chinese, Gothic and Modern Chairs* (1750-51) (see Peter Ward-Jackson, *English Furniture Designs of the Eighteenth Century*, London, 1958, pl. 180 – 'Parlour Chairs' dated 1766 – and p. 53).
Given by Mr Frank Green.

Height 100·2cm (3ft 3¾in)
Width   61·6cm (2ft 0¼in)

W.9-1932

76
CABINET ON STAND

Carved mahogany, the finials of gilt metal. Mid-eighteenth century. This piece was made to house a small Chinese cabinet with drawer-fronts veneered with tortoiseshell and set with pierced ivory plaques. From the Chinese Room at Claydon House, Buckinghamshire.
Given by Mr F. H. Reed.

Height 181·6cm (5ft 11½in)
Width   53·4cm (1ft 9in)

w.65-1953

77
COMMODE
Oak, with japanned decoration, brass mounts. About 1765. Although this piece owes much to French inspiration – the gilt bronze mounts are used in a typically French manner – the two doors masking the commode drawers behind are a peculiarly English feature.

Height 87·6cm (2ft 10½in)
Width 112·3cm (3ft 8½in)

W.61-1931

78
SETTEE
Carved mahogany; re-upholstered in Chinese painted satin. Mid-eighteenth century. In the 'Chinese' style. From Ingress Abbey, Kent and probably made for the second Earl of Bessborough, who bought Ingress in 1748.

Height 97·1cm (3ft 2½in)
Width 163·8cm (5ft 4½in)

W.7-1946

79

COMMODE

Japanned wood. About 1753. Possibly from the Chinese bedroom at Badminton, Gloucestershire. It seems reasonable to presume that this commode was part of the furniture that Thomas Chippendale is known to have provided for the fourth Duke of Beaufort at Badminton at this period. The bed illustrated in the frontispiece comes from the same room.

Height 98·4cm (3ft 3in)
Width 142·2cm (4ft 8in)

W.55-1952

80

BREAKFAST-TABLE

Mahogany. About 1755. This corresponds almost exactly with a design in Thomas Chippendale's *Director* (1st edition, 1754, pl. XXXIII). Given by the National Art-Collections Fund.

Height 72·4cm (2ft 4½in)
Width 58·5cm (1ft 11in)

w.64-1950

81
ARM-CHAIR
Mahogany, upholstered in modern silk. About 1760-70. From Bramshill, Hampshire. The deeply curved seat is unusual. Rotch Bequest.

Height 96·5cm (3ft 2$\frac{1}{8}$in)
Width   61cm (2ft)

W.46-1962

THE 'STRAWBERRY ROOM' FROM
LEE PRIORY, KENT
Painted pinewood. About 1782-90.
Lee priory was designed by James
Wyatt for Thomas Barrett, a close
friend of Horace Walpole. Walpole
much admired this 'Gothick' essay
which he called 'my Gothic child'
and wrote enthusiastically in 1790 to
Miss Mary Berry: 'I found
Mr Barrett's house complete, and the
most perfect thing ever formed! Such
taste, every inch, so well finished. . . .
I think if Strawberry were not its
parent, it would be jealous'.

Height 274·3cm (9ft 0¼in)
Width 220·9cm (7ft 3⅛in)

W.48-1953

FURNITURE IN THE 'STRAWBERRY ROOM'

Left:
ARTIST'S TABLE. Carved mahogany.
Third quarter of the eighteenth century.
In the style of Chippendale.
W.31-1912 (See fig. 84)

MIRROR. Carved pinewood, painted
white. Third quarter of the eighteenth
century. Given by Mr Roger Warner.
W.19-1961

CHAIR. Carved mahogany. Third
quarter of the eighteenth century.
W.13-1960

Right:
POLE-SCREEN. Carved mahogany.
Third quarter of the eighteenth century.
Given by Brigadier W. E. Clark, C.M.G.,
D.S.O., through the National
Art-Collections Fund.
W.34-1959 (See fig. 69)

PAIR OF CHAIRS. Carved mahogany.
Third quarter of the eighteenth
century. Given by Messrs Frank
Partridge and Sons.
W.23-1956

83

KETTLE-STAND

Carved mahogany. Third quarter of the eighteenth century. On one side there is a sliding panel for supporting a bowl or cup to catch drips from the kettle spout. Given by Brigadier W. E. Clark, C.M.G., D.S.O., through the National Art-Collections Fund.

Height 67·3cm (2ft 2½in)
Width   33cm (1ft 1in)

W.7-1961

84
ARTIST'S TABLE
Carved mahogany. Third quarter of the eighteenth century. A design in Ince and Mayhew's *Universal System of Household Furniture*, (1762-63) is similar to this table.

Height   80cm (2ft 7½in)
Width   91·4cm (3ft)

W.31-1912

85
READING-TABLE
Carved mahogany. Made in 1770 by William France for Robert Adam's library at Kenwood. The bill from France to Lord Mansfield, dated 4th December 1770, reads: 'For a large mahogany Reading Stand on a stout pillar and claw, with a screw nutt, worked very true capable of screwing to rise 10 inches if required. The whole of very good mahogany and the pillar and claw richly carved'. Although Adam supervised closely the furnishing of a number of the houses that he decorated – as at Osterley and Harewood – this table demonstrates that he did not always do so, for the marked rococo flavour of this piece is very different from the strictly measured neo-classical rhythms of Adam's library at Kenwood.

Height 76·2cm (2ft 6in)
Width 65·4cm (2ft 1¾in)

W.202-1923

THE LIBRARY AT OSTERLEY PARK
HOUSE

Designed by Robert Adam in 1766. The inset paintings are by Antonio Zucchi, A.R.A. The suite of furniture, of mahogany inlaid with satinwood and other woods and embellished with gilt bronze mounts, comprises eight arm-chairs, two writing-tables and a pedestal writing-table. It was probably designed and made by John Linnell about 1775. (See Eileen Harris, *The Furniture of Robert Adam*, 1963, p.93).

87
THE EATING ROOM AT OSTERLEY
PARK HOUSE

Designed by Robert Adam about 1767. The inset paintings are by Antonio Zucchi, A.R.A. The set of ten lyre-back chairs is after a design of about 1767 by Robert Adam, now in the Soane Museum, Vol. 17, no. 93. The sideboard is after a design by Adam, dated 1767, now in the Soane Museum, Vol. 17, no. 7. (See Eileen Harris, *ibid.*) The pair of urns on either side of the chimney-piece were probably made by John Linnell, who made a closely similar pair for Shardeloes, Buckinghamshire, and who is known to have made furniture for Osterley.
(See figs. 86 and 88)

THE TAPESTRY ROOM AT
OSTERLEY PARK HOUSE
The tapestries specially woven for the room at the Gobelins works in Paris and dated 1775, are signed by Neilson (director of the low-warp *atelier* at the Gobelins) in the panel over the fireplace. They portray scenes from *Les Amours des Dieux* by Boucher, framed in simulated gold medallions on a crimson ground. The chairs and the settee, upholstered in tapestry *en suite*, have designs from a series by Boucher known as *Les Enfants Jardiniers*. The firescreen frame, though of a later date, is made up from a fragment of tapestry taken from behind the mirror on the window-side. Thomas Moore made the carpet to a design by Robert Adam (Soane Museum, Vol. 17, no. 187) dated 8th July 1775. The stand, one of a pair, in the corner, was designed by Robert Adam (Soane Museum, Vol. 17, no. 62) on 13th May 1776 and supports an incense-burner of later date.

89
DRAWING-ROOM
With fireplace and ceiling from No. 5 The Adelphi Terrace, London. Designed by Robert and James Adam and occupied by David Garrick. About 1770. Fireplace given by the National Art-Collections Fund; ceiling by the Adelphi Development Company.

W.42 & 43-1936

FURNITURE IN THE ADELPHI ROOM

Left:
ARM-CHAIR (See fig. 101).
W.21-1922

SIDE-TABLE. Carved and gilt pine, the top veneered with painted satinwood. About 1780. One of a pair. Lent by the Lady Lever Art Gallery, Port Sunlight.

ARM-CHAIR. Carved mahogany. About 1780.
1458-1904

Centre:
ARM-CHAIR. Carved mahogany. About 1780. Rotch Bequest.
W.27-1962

PAIR OF DINING TABLES. Carved mahogany, the top covered with figured veneer. About 1770-75.
W.37-1929

ARM-CHAIR. Carved mahogany. About 1775. Originally one of a set of nine. Given by Commander Walter N. Westhead, R.N.V.R.
W.2-1946

CHAIR. Carved mahogany. About 1785.
W.68-1935

Right:
COMMODE. Painted satinwood with rosewood inlay. About 1790.
636-1870

WALL LIGHT. Carved pinewood, wire and composition, all gilt. About 1790. One of a pair. Hudson Bequest.
W.20-1937

PAIR OF CANDLESTANDS. (See fig. 95a)
W.36 & a-1936

OVERMANTEL MIRROR. Pinewood, carved and gilt. From Bradbourne, Kent, which was decorated in 1774.
W.66-1938

90
ARM-CHAIR
Carved and gilded beechwood, upholstered in crimson silk. From a suite of furniture originally consisting of eight arm-chairs and four sofas designed in 1764 by Robert Adam for Sir Lawrence Dundas's London house at 19 Arlington Street. (The designs are in the Soane Museum, Vol. 17, no. 74). Adam charged £5 'To a design of sofa chairs for the salon' on the 18th of July, 1765. The suite was executed by Thomas Chippendale and his bill, for '8 large Arm Chairs exceeding richly carved in the Antick manner and Gilt in oil Gold Stuffed and cover'd with your own Damask and Strong Castors on the feet' came to £160. The four sofas cost £216 and all were provided with leather cases lined with flannel and crimson checked linen covers. The bill was dated 9th July 1765.

Three sofas and four chairs still remain at Aske Hall, Yorkshire, the seat of the Marquess of Zetland, descendant of Sir Lawrence Dundas.

This chair, which is one of Adam's most successful furniture designs, is stamped VII.

Height 105·9cm (3ft 6in)
Width   77·4cm (2ft 6½in)

W.1-1937

91
WALL DECORATION
Detail of wall decoration in the Glass Drawing Room from Northumberland House, London. Designed by Robert Adam. About 1771, see p.12. This room will be the subject of the first book in a new series devoted to the period rooms in the museum.

W.3-1955

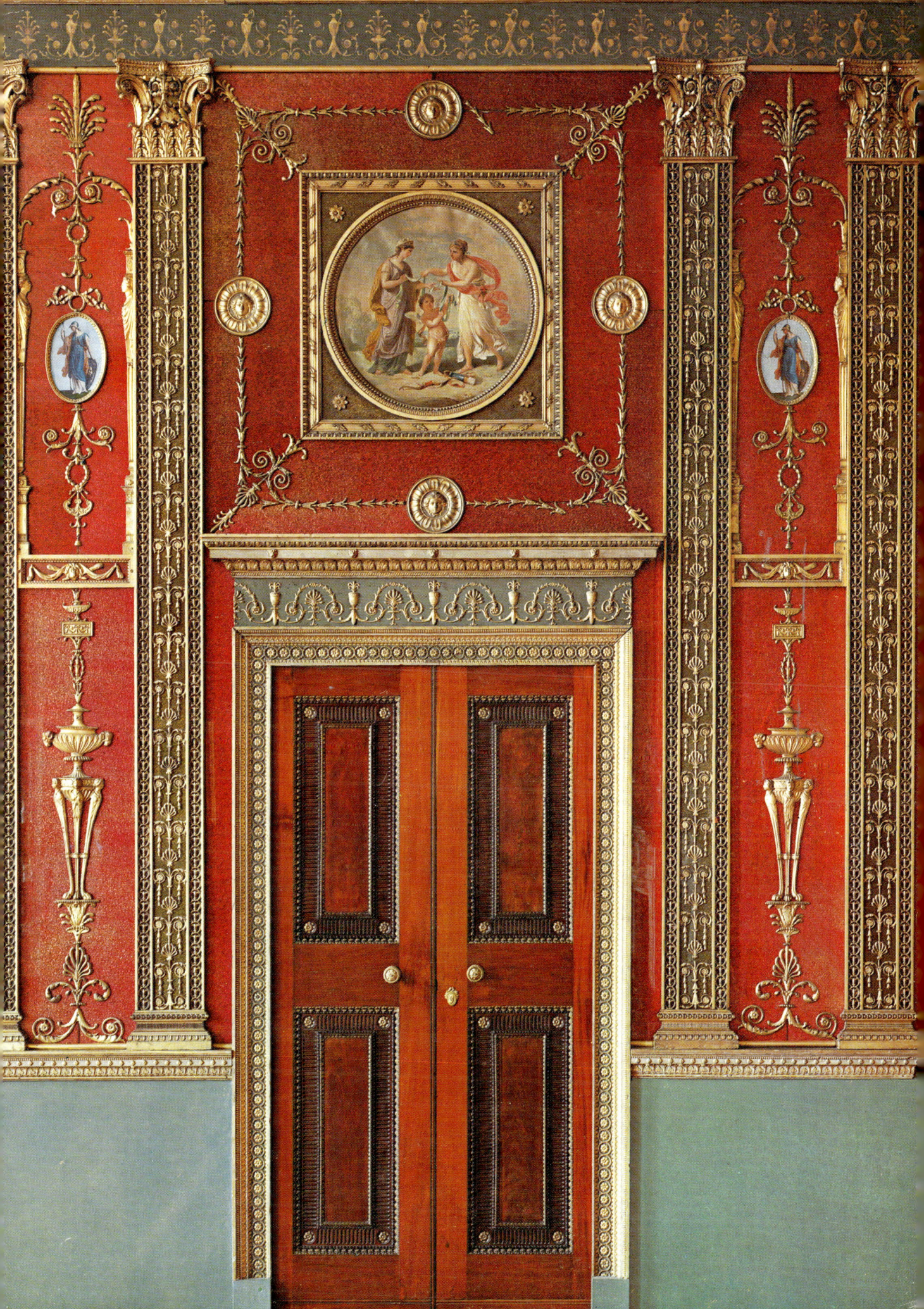

92

SIDEBOARD PEDESTAL

Carved mahogany. About 1765. One of a pair. The urns are fitted with lead wine coolers and one pedestal has a removable drawer divided into four compartments for bottles. Pedestals of this type were apparently introduced in conjunction with sideboard tables about 1760. See Thomas Chippendale's *Director* (3rd edition, 1762, pl. CL). Given by Mr John A. Tulk.

Height 162·6cm (5ft 3¾in)
Width 50·2cm (1ft 7¾in)

w.38-1934

93

CANDELABRUM AND PEDESTAL (both one of a pair). About 1765. The candelabrum of fluor-spar ('Blue John') with ormolu mounts. Made by Matthew Boulton (1778-1807) for Sir Lawrence Dundas, Moor Park, Hertfordshire. The pedestal was probably made by Thomas Chippendale, to a design by Robert Adam, also for Sir Lawrence. Given by the National Art-Collections Fund.

Candelabrum Height 82·5cm (2ft 8½in)

W.23-1934

Pedestal Height 137·1cm (4ft 6in)

W.24-1934

94
GIRANDOLE
Frame of carved and gilded wood. One of a set of six in the Long Gallery at Osterley Park House. Probably made by John Linnell, with several alterations, from a design of 1770 by Robert Adam, now in the Soane Museum, Vol. 20, no. 36. (See Eileen Harris, *The Furniture of Robert Adam*, London, 1963).

Height 228·6cm (7ft 6in)
Width 111·8cm (3ft 8in)

95a
CANDLE-STAND
Carved mahogany and pine wood, painted blue and ivory, the original colours. One of a pair. Designed by Robert Adam for the Eating Room of Sir Watkin Williams-Wynn's house, No. 20 St. James's Square, which was being built between 1771 and 1774.

Height 121·9cm (4ft)

W.36-1946

95b
CANDLE-STAND
Carved and gilt wood. About 1770. One of a pair. In the Adam style. The original provenance of these splendid stands is not known, but they came to the Museum from the collection of Lord Brownlow.

Height   172cm (5ft 7¾in)
Width   53·4cm (1ft 9in)

W.72-1923

95c
CANDLE-STAND
Pinewood, carved and gilded. About 1770.

Height 138·3cm (4ft 6½in)

W.37-1937

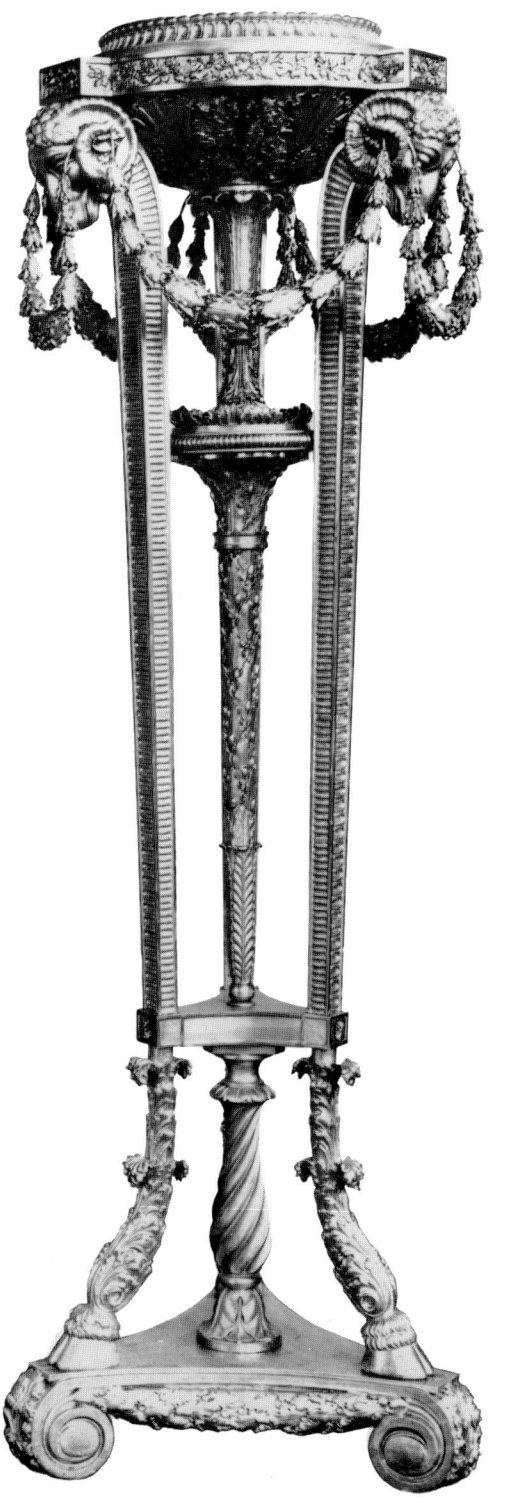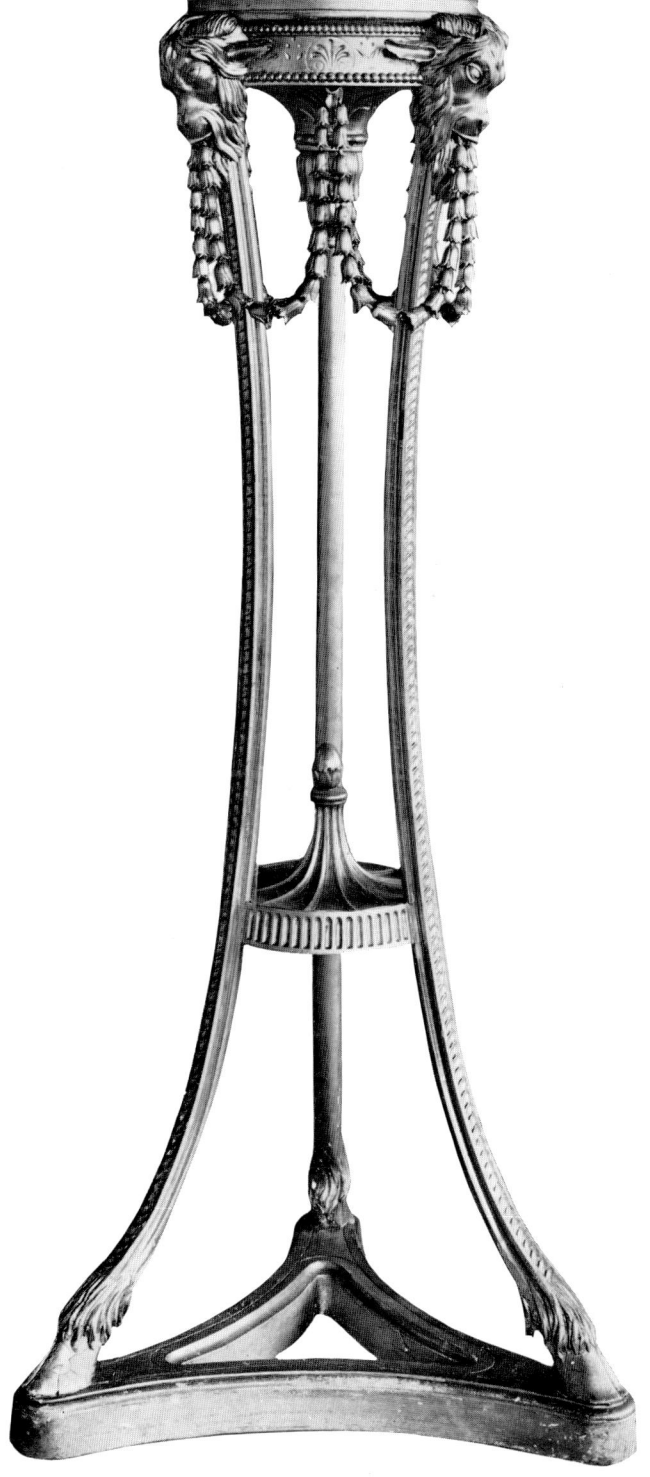

96
ARM-CHAIR
Carved and gilt wood, upholstered in modern silk. About 1775. This chair, which is of particularly fine quality, shows marked French influence and is similar to a drawing by John Linnell in the collection of his designs referred to in the Introduction (Department of Prints and Drawings; pressmark 92.D.26., E.78-1929). Given by the Ministry of Public Building and Works.

Height 103·5cm (3ft 5in)
Width   63·5cm (2ft 1in)

W.42-1946

97
CABINET

Marquetry of satinwood, rosewood and other woods, set with marble intarsia panels, and with mounts of gilded brass. The marble panels signed and dated *Baccio Cappelli fecit anno 1709 Fiorenza*. This cabinet was designed by Robert Adam for Elizabeth, Duchess of Manchester to provide a setting for the eleven panels of marble intarsia. The original drawing is in the Soane Museum and is dated 1st June 1771. The cabinet was made by Ince and Mayhew, while Matthew Boulton designed and cast the mounts. He wrote to the firm on 6th April 1775 concerning 'ornaments for the Duchess of Manchester's cabinet' which 'will be compleat for gilding in about 9 days when we shall immediately as they are ready forward them to you in order to try how they fit as we think it best so to do, before they are gilt for fear there should be any alterations to make after (when considered that the gilding parts will not delay them above 3 or 4 days after we receive them back) we are sorry it has not been in our power to complete them sooner and hope our delay will be no great disappointment'. This piece of furniture was designed solely as a vehicle for displaying the marble panels; it has little practical function, having no drawers, and access to the interior is only through doors in the angled ends.

Height 188cm (6ft $2\frac{1}{4}$in)
Width 177·8cm (5ft 10in)

W.43-1949

98
CARD-TABLE
Carved mahogany. About 1765-70.
Bequeathed by Mr F. D. Brown.

Height 71·8cm (2ft 4¼in)
Width 90·1cm (2ft 11½in)

W.1-1927

99
DRESSING COMMODE
Mahogany, inlaid with satinwood, the mouldings ebonized. About 1775. The top drawer is fitted with an interior slide covered with green baize and giving access to interior horizontal fittings consisting of a tilting and sliding mirror and lidded compartments. This is a particularly good example of the anglicising of a French form, in which the intricacies of the French original – with its gilt metal mounts and marquetry – have been simplified into this reticent but none the less elegant piece of furniture.

Height 87·6cm (2ft 10½in)
Width 105·4cm (3ft 5⅞in)

W.55-1937

100

CABINET

Mahogany, inlaid with satinwood.
About 1775. The upper stage of this
cabinet follows very closely a design
by John Linnell. Bequeathed by
Sir Herbert Mitchell, K.C.V.O.

Height 215·9cm (7ft 0¾in)
Width 111·1cm (3ft 8in)

W.50-1936

101
ARM-CHAIR
Carved mahogany; modern
upholstery. About 1775.

Height 91·4cm (3ft)
Width 62·8cm (2ft 0¾in)

W.21-1922

102
ARM-CHAIR
Carved mahogany upholstered in modern yellow damask. Third quarter of the eighteenth century. In the 'French' taste. Given by Brigadier W. E. Clark, C.M.G., D.S.O., through the National Art-Collections Fund.

Height 97·1cm (3ft 2½in)
Width 71·2cm (2ft 4in)

w.8-1961

103
COMMODE
Mahogany, with marquetry of rosewood, satinwood, tulip and holly, ormolu mounts. About 1772. Made in the 'French' taste by John Cobb of 72 St. Martin's Lane, upholsterer to George III, and very similar to one for which the bill exists dated 1772 at Corsham, Wiltshire. Cobb was, until 1765-66, the partner of William Vile. (See figs. 33, 34 and 35).

Height   87·6cm (2ft 10½in)
Width   111·1cm (3ft 8in)

W.30-1937

104
COMMODE
Satinwood with laburnum banding
and marquetry of various woods.
About 1775. Possibly attributable to
John Cobb (see fig. 103) and in the
French taste. Given by
Mrs. H. H. Mulliner.

Height 86·4cm (2ft 10in)
Width 74·9cm (2ft 5½in)

w.88-1924

105
TROPHY
Detail of trophy in right-hand door
of the commode illustrated in fig. 104.

w.88-1924

106a

DRESSING-TABLE

Mahogany overlaid with marquetry of satinwood, laburnum and other woods. About 1770. Given by Mrs H. H. Mulliner.

Height 71·2cm (2ft 4in)
Width 75·6cm (2ft 5¾in)

w.89-1924

106b
Fig. 106a open.

107
PEDESTAL DRESSING-TABLE
Mahogany with kingwood veneer and marquetry of various woods. About 1775. This type, termed a 'Buroe Dressing Table' is illustrated in Chippendale's *Director* and other publications of the period. In style, the table resembles the inlaid furniture made by Chippendale and Haig & Co. for Harewood House, Yorkshire. Given by Mr Frank Partridge through the National Art-Collections Fund.

Height 78·8cm (2ft 7in)
Width   125·6cm (4ft 1½in)

W.55-1928

108
COMMODE
Harewood inlaid with satinwood, tulip, burr walnut and holly. About 1782. Attributed to William Moore of Dublin and very similar to another at Welbeck Abbey made by Moore for the third Duke of Portland in 1782, when he was Viceroy of Ireland. Moore had been apprenticed to Ince & Mayhew and it is interesting to compare the marquetry of this piece with that of the Duchess of Manchester's cabinet (fig. 97).

Height   88·3cm (2ft 10¾in)
Width   141·6cm (4ft 7¾in)

W.56-1925

109
LONG-CASE CLOCK
Carved mahogany case with brass face partly silvered. About 1780. Movement by William Barker, Wigan. This clock and fig. 110 by provincial makers, have features that would have gone out of fashion in London somewhat earlier. The general proportions lack some of the elegance of the best London productions, but the craftsmanship is good.

Height 236·2cm (7ft 9¼in)
Width   54·6cm (1ft 9½in)

w.81-1910

110
LONG-CASE CLOCK
Carved mahogany, with gilded brass mounts. About 1775. Movement by Davidson/Ecclesham.
Given by Mr Eric M. Browett.

Height 241·2cm (7ft 11½in)
Width 61cm (2ft)

W.50-1937

111a

DRESSING-TABLE

Mahogany veneered with harewood. Late eighteenth century. Dressing-tables of similar type are shown in Hepplewhite's *Cabinet-Maker and Upholsterer's Guide* (3rd edition, 1794, pl. 72), and Sheraton's *Cabinet-Maker and Upholsterer's Drawing-Book* (3rd edition, 1802, pl. 20). Given by Mr S. M. Messer.

Height 92·6cm (3ft 0½in)
Width 63·5cm (2ft 1in)

W.14-1959

111b
Fig. 111a open.

112

URN-TABLE

Satinwood, with painted decoration.
On the far side is a small hinged flap.
Mark: *M. Gregson Liverpool* 1790; for
Matthew Gregson (b. 1749, d. 1824),
upholsterer and antiquary. Bequeathed
by Lady Isabella D. Wilson.

Height 72·4cm (2ft 4½in)
Width 36·8cm (1ft 2½in)

W.45-1935

113
PEMBROKE TABLE
Satinwood with marquetry of various woods. Late eighteenth century. Given in memory of Lady Henriques.

Height 73·7cm (2ft 5in)
Width 72·4cm (2ft 4½in)

w.6-1959

114a
SIDE-TABLE
Pine wood, painted and gilt.
One of a pair. About 1780.

Height 81·3cm (2ft 8in)
Width 116·1cm (3ft 9¾in)

349a-1871

114b
The top of fig. 114a painted in the style of Angelica Kauffmann.

115a

SIDE-TABLE

Of gilt wood with painted top. About 1793. One of a pair of which the companion is in the Metropolitan Museum, New York. The table is stamped 'G.IV.R' on the back, and the tables are believed to have been at Carlton House. This, and their general style suggest that they may have been designed by Henry Holland who was responsible for much of the furnishing of Carlton House.

Height 80·6cm (2ft 7¾in)
Width 117·4cm (3ft 10¼in)

W.42-1928

115b
Top of fig. 115a. The central panel is after Guido Reni's *Aurora* in the Casino of the Rospigliosi Palace, Rome.

116
ARM-CHAIR
Satinwood, painted in polychrome.
One of a set of 18 chairs made in 1790
by George Seddon and Sons and
J. Shackleton for D. Tupper, Hauteville
House, Guernsey. The original bill
reads '18 Satinwood Elbow Chairs
round fronts & hollow can'd seats
neatly Japanned – ornamented with
roses in back and peacock feather
border . . . @ 73/6 ea . . . 66.3.0'.

Height 92·6cm (3ft 2½in)
Width   58cm (1ft 10⅞in)

W.1-1968

117
ARM-CHAIR
Mahogany with painted decoration.
Modern upholstery. About 1785.

Height 95·8cm (3ft 1¼in)
Width 58·5cm (1ft 10in)

w.52-1946

118
ARM-CHAIR
Carved mahogany with metal details;
upholstered in modern silk. About 1775.

Height 87·6cm (2ft 10½in)
Width 58·5cm (1ft 11in)

45-1869

119
ARM-CHAIR
Carved mahogany; modern upholstery.
About 1783-90.
Given by Mr Donald Gunn.

Height 87·9cm (2ft 10$\frac{5}{8}$in)
Width 62·2cm (2ft 0$\frac{1}{2}$in)

w.64-1930

120a & b
PAIR OF KNIFE BOXES
Yew veneer, with silver mounts.
About 1770.

Height 39·3cm (1ft 3½in)
Width   26cm (10¼in)

w.90 & a-1926

121a-c
TEA-CADDIES

Inlaid; (a) harewood; (b) satinwood; (c) walnut; about 1790. When tea was first imported into England it was extremely expensive and cost from sixteen to fifty shillings a pound. It was the practice to lock the caddy when not in use.

The word 'caddy' is a corruption of 'catty' (Kāti), a weight used in the Eastern Archipelago and China, equal to a little more than a pound avoirdupois. The term caddy came into the English language between 1754, the date of Chippendale's first *Director* (which lists only tea-chests) and 1788, the date of the publication of Hepplewhite's *The Cabinet-Maker and Upholsterer's Guide*, where both tea-chests and tea-caddies are illustrated. In most cases the tea-caddy was partitioned for black and green tea or fitted with canisters for two varieties, which were blended to suit the taste of the drinker. 121 (c) is stamped: *Gillows Lancaster*.

Given by Mr Thomas Sutton.

Height (a) 12·1cm (4⅝in)
      (b) 12·7cm (5in)
      (c) 10·9cm (4⅜in)

w.98, 108, 101-1919

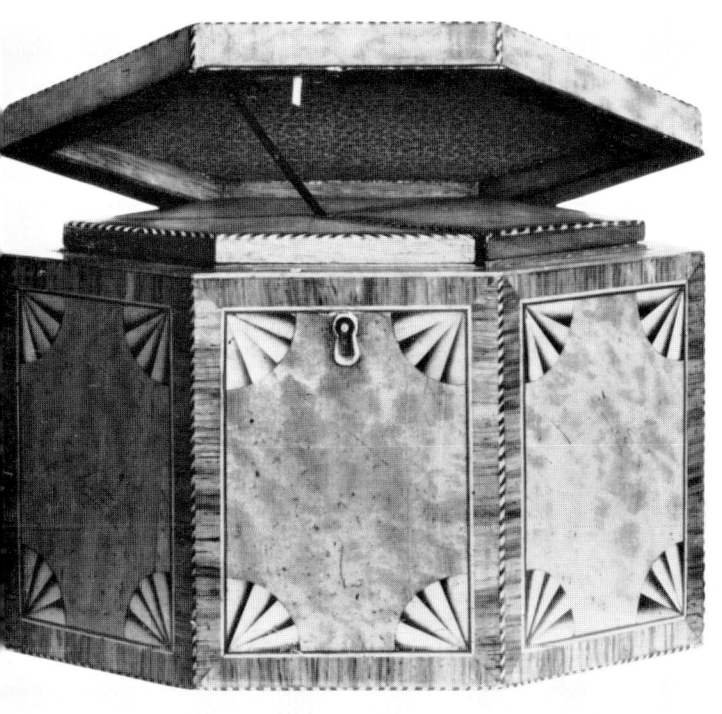

122
KNIFE-CASE
(Shown open). Satinwood, with painted decoration. About 1780.

Height 74·9cm (2ft 5½in)
Diameter 34·2cm (1ft 1½in)

W.28-1912

123

TERRESTRIAL GLOBE
On mahogany stand, the stand about 1800. One of a pair by W. and T. M. Bardin. Globe dated 1843 and dedicated to Sir Joseph Banks, President of the Royal Society.
Given by Mr Murray Marks.

Height of stand   6·3cm (1ft 11¾in)
Diameter of globe 45·7cm (1ft 6in)

w.52-1916

124

DRESSING CASE AND STAND
Laburnum or possibly olive wood.
Third quarter of the eighteenth century.
The lid contains a writing leaf. The
internal fittings include five lidded
compartments; there were originally
four small metal containers for ink
and toiletries etc. at the corners, of
which one survives.
Rotch Bequest.

Height 86·4cm (2ft 10in)
Width 40·7cm (1ft 4in)

w.26-1962

125
BAROMETER AND THERMOMETER
About 1800. Mahogany case, brass mouldings and painted glass. Instruments by John Russell of Falkirk, watchmaker to George, Prince of Wales. Two very similar barometers are at Buckingham Palace.

Height 121·9cm (4ft)
Width   33cm (1ft 1in)

w.18-1936

126
SECRETARY-BOOKCASE
Satinwood with inlay of various woods,
painted decoration. About 1790.
Given by Sir Claude Phillips.

Height 208·3cm (6ft 10in)
Width   132·1cm (4ft 4in)

W.121-1924

127
BUREAU-BOOKCASE
Inlaid Satinwood. Late eighteenth century. The cylinder-top of this desk is a French feature, which was adopted by the English towards the end of the eighteenth century. One of the very earliest examples of this feature is on Reisener's famous *Bureau du Roi* at Versailles.

Height 213·4cm (6ft 11¾in)
Width   98·4cm (3ft 3in)

W.84-1910

128
MIRROR
Pinewood frame, carved and gilded with convex glass. About 1800.

Height 259cm (8ft 4in)
Width 105·9cm (3ft 6in)

w.85-1926

129
MIRROR
Carved and gilded pinewood frame.
About 1810.

Height 109·9cm (3ft 7¾in)
Width   66·1cm (2ft 1¾in)

w.60-1937

130
LIBRARY STEPS
Mahogany. About 1790. On the underside of the top is the maker's label inscribed *Hervé fecit No. 32 John Street, Tottenham Court Road*. This was Francis Hervé, who worked for George, Prince of Wales, at Carlton House between 1783-89.

Height 233·6cm (7ft 8in)
Width 55·9cm (1ft 10in)

W.7-1932

131
LIBRARY TABLE
Mahogany veneered with sabicu wood. About 1810. Carved with emblems and symbols of Architecture, Comedy, Tragedy, Peace, War, Medicine and Literature. Now at Osterley Park House.

Height 78·8cm (2ft 7in)
Width   136·5cm (4ft 5$\frac{3}{4}$in)

w.28-1938

132
SIDEBOARD
About 1800. Carved mahogany. The brass rail should possess a curtain.

Height 93·3cm (3ft 1in)
Width 213·4cm (7ft)

W.41-1950

133
DRESSING-TABLE
Carved mahogany, inlaid with ebony.
Conforms to a design dated 18th
July 1805 in George Smith's *Collection of Designs for Household Furniture* (1808), pl. XXII. He writes that it contains five drawers without any dressing apparatus, and that the ornaments are to be formed in an inlay of ebony or carved in the mahogany. The drawers, made without handles, are to be locked by spring catches and released by springs behind. The maker has carefully adhered to these directions. Smith's design was in turn inspired by a drawing made by Charles Heathcote Tatham of an altar 'in a chapel near Rome'. (See Clifford Musgrave, *Regency Furniture*. London, 1961, p. 52 and pl. 1.)

Height 71·2cm (2ft 4in)
Width 116·8cm (3ft 10in)

W.25-1946

134
STAND
Carved mahogany. About 1810. One of a pair. It closely resembles a stand shown in the extreme left of a design by Thomas Hope of Deepdene, *Household Furniture and Interior Decoration*, (London, 1807, p. 11), and repeated on pl. 15 fig. 1, where the stand is described as 'a tripod stand supported by chimaeras'.

Height 83·9cm (2ft 9in)
Width 50·8cm (1ft 8in)

W.35-1946

135
LIBRARY-TABLE
Rosewood with carved and gilded gesso decoration. About 1810. The top covered with leather. Similar to a table illustrated in Thomas Hope's *Household Furniture*, (1808), pl. 32.

Height 78·8cm (2ft 7in)
Width   105·9cm (3ft 6in)

w.49-1946

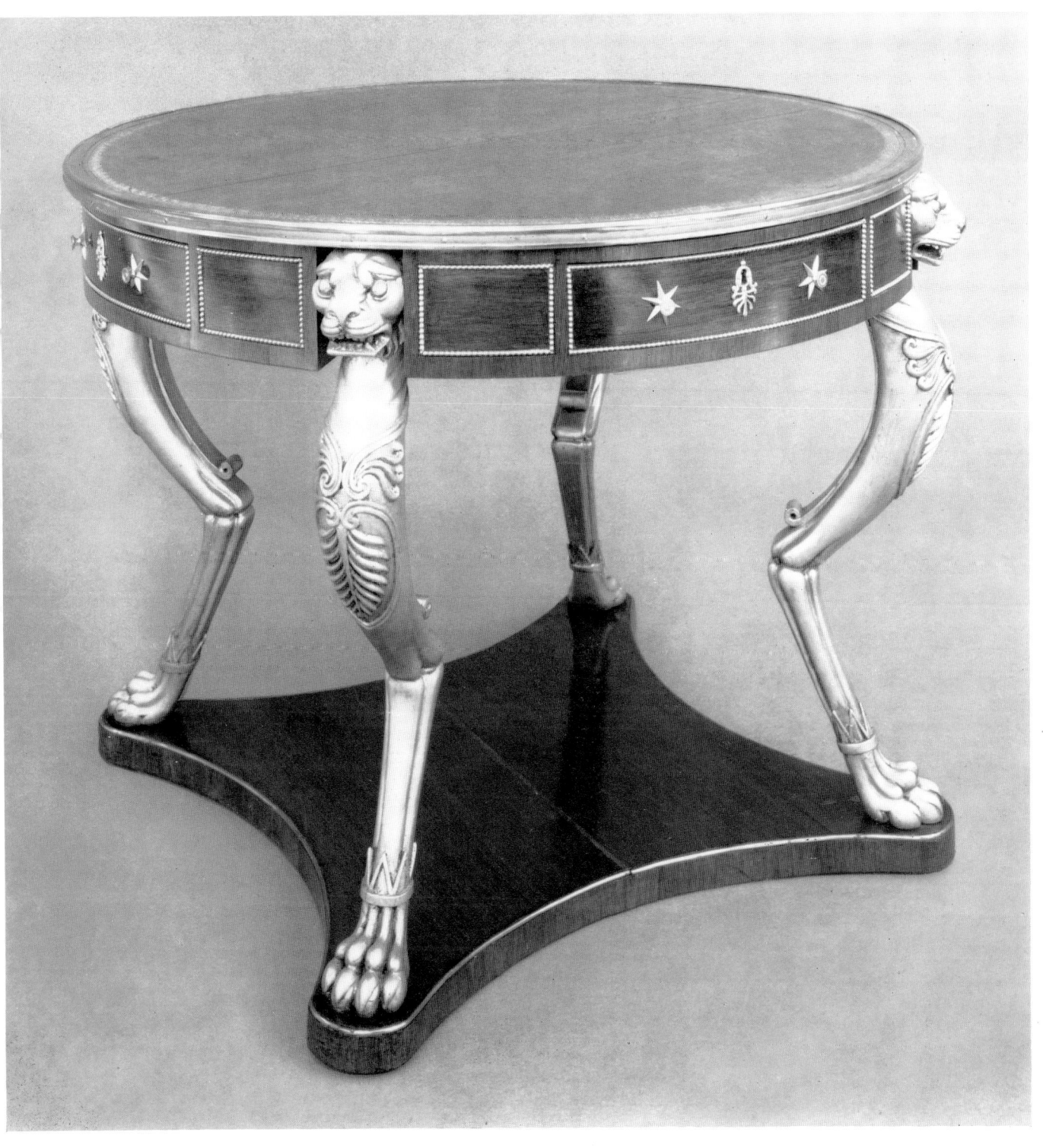

136
SETTEE
Carved and gilt beechwood, upholstered in modern silk. It formed part of a set of twelve arm-chairs and two settees made by Gillow, London, in 1805 for Colonel Hughes of Kinmel Park, Denbighshire. The Lancaster firm of Gillow established a branch in London in 1761.

Height 82·5cm (2ft 8½in)
Width 203·2cm (6ft 8in)

W.38-1930

137
SECRETARY
Mahogany veneered with zebrawood and bands of satinwood. The masks and feet are of brass. Behind the glass are watercolours of scenes on the Clyde, signed *J. Baynes, 1808*.

Height 158·7cm (5ft 2½in)
Width 78·1cm (2ft 6¾in)

W.15-1930

138

HANGING CABINET

Mahogany inlaid with brass, metal and various woods. About 1810-20. The crocodile is sometimes said to be a reference to Nelson's victory of the Nile (1797) but this seems improbable. It may be a crest or a manifestation of the Egyptian taste then prevailing. The cabinet also displays classical and neo-Gothic features.

Height 192·2cm (6ft 2½in)
Width 115·2cm (3ft 9⅜in)

w.63-1935

139
CABINET
Satinwood with inlaid banding,
painted detail and gilt brass mounts.
About 1820. Given by Mr F. H. Reed.

Height 128·2cm (4ft 2½in)
Width 73·7cm (2ft 5in)

w.64-1953

140

SECRETARY

Rosewood with satinwood stringing and brass mounts. About 1810. The piece bears a label: 'Manufactured and sold by John McLane [sic] and Son, Pancras Street, Tottenham Court Road and 58, Upper Marylebone Street, Portland Place'. McClean's name appears in Thomas Sheraton's list of cabinet-makers in the *Cabinet Dictionary* (London, 1803), where the design for a work or 'pouch table' is said to 'be taken from one executed by Mr McClean in Marylebone Street . . . . . who finishes these small articles in the neatest manner . . .'. McClean was also noted for having on sale 'elegant Parisian furniture'. The present piece has several markedly French features which may well be the result of McClean having studied the French furniture that passed through his hands.
Murray Bequest.

Height 146·6cm (4ft 9¾in)
Width   92·2cm (3ft 0½in)

W.10-1944

141
CHAIR
Beech, japanned black and gilded.
The honeysuckle motif and cresting
are of gilt metal. First quarter of the
nineteenth century.
Caned seat supporting a squab
covered with modern silk. One from a
set of twelve. Lady Glyn Bequest.

Height 86·4cm (2ft 10in)
Width 45·7cm (1ft 6in)

w.27-1958

142
TEA POY
Rosewood, with parquetry of various woods (Tunbridge Ware). About 1825. Brass feet and castors.
F. L. Lucas Bequest.

Height 78·8cm (2ft 7in)
Width 44·4cm (1ft 5½in)

W.5-1931

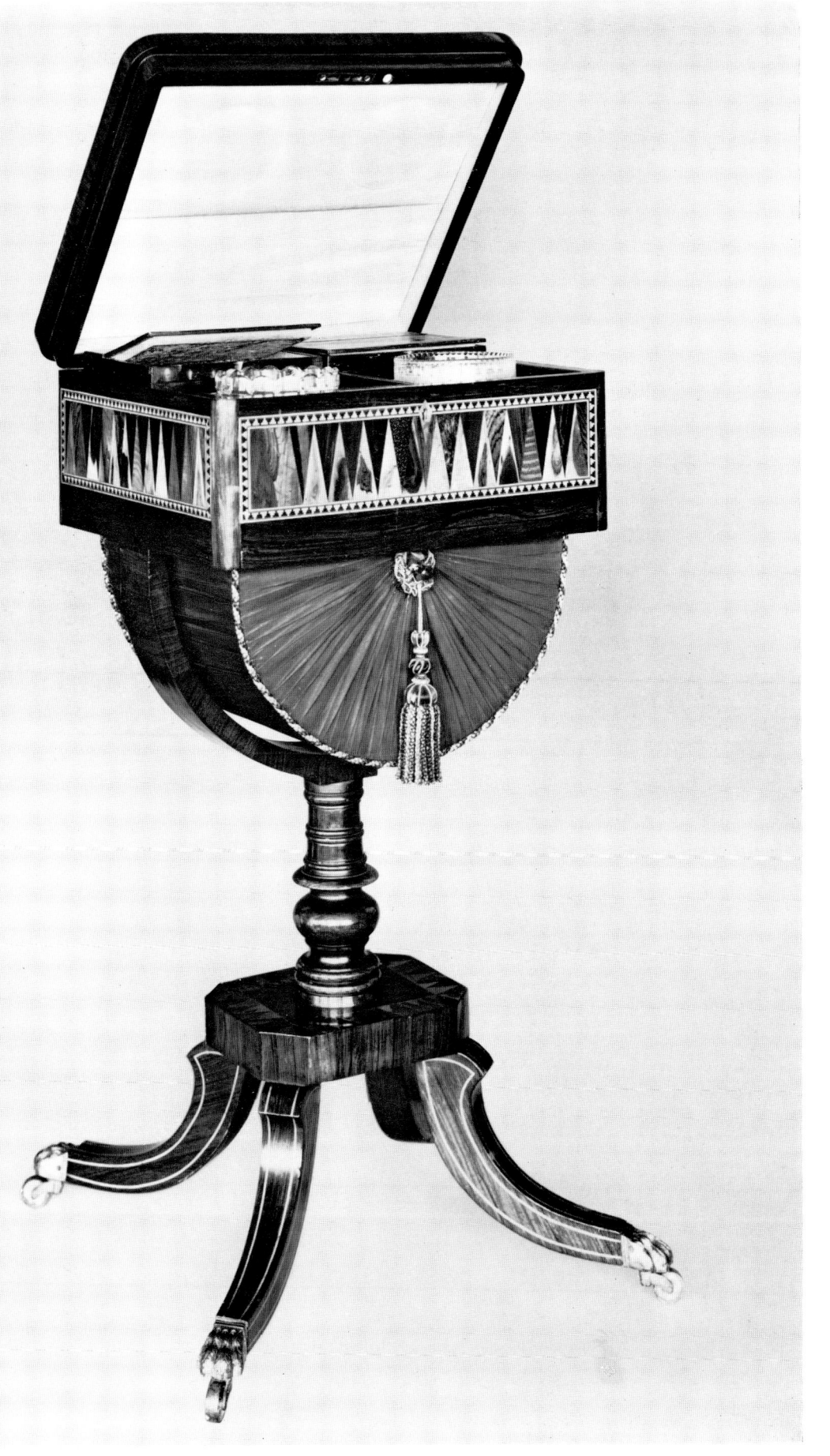

143
PEDESTAL TABLE
Coromandel wood veneer and lacquered brass mounts. The top frames an engraving of the design, made about 1820, by Thomas Stothard, R.A. (1755-1834) for the Wellington Shield now at Apsley House. About 1820.
At Osterley Park House.

Height 75·5cm (2ft 6½in)
Diameter 121cm (4ft)

144
SIDEBOARD
Rosewood inlaid with brass. About 1820. The sarcophagus-shaped urns contain knife boxes.
Given by Lady Neville.

Height 138·3cm (4ft 6½in)
Width   188cm (6ft 2in)

W.149-1923

Dd 134904 K32